PRAISE FOR *CLASH OF KINGDOMS*

"If you're fascinated by end times prophecy—and who isn't?—you've found the right book. In this compact but thorough treatise, Charlie Dyer and Mark Tobey deftly interweave ancient Scriptures with tomorrow's headlines and explain all the nuances of all the players. You'll learn more than you thought there was to know and come away from the easily read narrative thoroughly informed. But better than that, you will have seen the trace of God's hand in everything that has happened around our globe since time began."

—Jerry Jenkins, novelist and biographer, writer
of the Left Behind series for Tim LaHaye

"If the prophecies of the Bible concerning the end times seem like a puzzle you can't complete, this book is the box top. Each chapter is a carefully cut piece with the edges and the colors designed to help one see the big picture of God's prophetic plan. Charlie Dyer and Mark Tobey avoid the twin dangers of the overly sensational and the under-preparedness that so often is present in the study of prophecy."

—Dr. Mark L. Bailey, president,
Dallas Theological Seminary

"The world is aflame. Terrorism, militarism, nuclear proliferation. It should not surprise anyone that the crises in the Middle East, Europe, and Russia were addressed thousands of years ago in the Scriptures. Moreover, no interpreters are more skillful than Charlie Dyer and Mark Tobey in explaining what the Bible reveals about this clash of kingdoms and the true hope readers can have despite a world filled with terror."

—Dr. Michael Rydelnik, professor of Jewish Studies,
Moody Bible Institute; Host and Bible teacher on
Moody Radio's *Open Line with Dr. Michael Rydelnik*

P9-CEU-741

"Today's headlines repeatedly expose how unstable our world has become. If we can't get a handle on the accelerated pace of global change from a biblical perspective, we could be filled with fear, even as believers. But Jesus never intended us to live that way. That's why you need to read *Clash of Kingdoms* by Charles Dyer and Mark Tobey. This book takes the puzzle pieces of today's news and synchronizes them perfectly with the Word of God. I'm recommending it to everyone, including my pastor friends. This book is a wake-up call for every believer in Christ. It reminds us all that Jesus is on the throne, and that *things are not falling apart, they're falling in to place.*"

—TOM DOYLE, VICE PRESIDENT, E3PARTNERS
AND MIDDLE EAST DIRECTOR

"During my days as a student at Dallas Theological Seminary, Charlie Dyer was one of my favorite professors. His reservoir of knowledge filled my head, and his passion for God and His Word filled my heart. He made the Old Testament prophets come alive. Through his books, I still have the privilege to learn from him today. I read everything he writes. You should too."

—DR. MARK HITCHCOCK, SENIOR PASTOR, FAITH BIBLE
CHURCH, EDMOND, OKLAHOMA, AND ASSOCIATE PROFESSOR
OF BIBLE EXPOSITION, DALLAS THEOLOGICAL SEMINARY

"Dyer and Tobey have provided a clear presentation of key prophetic issues and how they relate to our own day. Since the Bible lays out a detailed and clear road map of events that will take place after the rapture, Dyer and Tobey have shown how the stage is being set in our own day in preparation for that future fulfillment. Anyone interested in Bible prophecy would be interested in reading this well-written account of how the present relates to God's plan for the future."

—DR. THOMAS ICE, EXECUTIVE DIRECTOR OF
THE PRE-TRIB RESEARCH CENTER

"Jesus predicted that in the last days the nations of the world would find themselves in a state of perplexity (Luke 21:25). Today, we see Christ's prophecy coming to pass perhaps as never before as geopolitical observers routinely scratch their heads with bewilderment at the perplexing and seemingly out of control international scene. Yet, as these very events are examined through the lens of Scripture, one need not be gripped by fear since they are fitting into a prophetic scenario long ago predicted in the pages of God's holy Word. As shown by Dr. Charles Dyer and Mark Tobey in *Clash of Kingdoms*, God has not lost control of a world that, from the human point of view, seems to be spinning wildly out of control. This book is required reading for those seeking to see God's divine hand in today's chaotic headlines."

—DR. ANDY WOODS, SENIOR PASTOR, SUGAR LAND BIBLE CHURCH; PROFESSOR, COLLEGE OF BIBLE STUDIES

CLASH OF KINGDOMS

CLASH OF KINGDOMS

WHAT THE BIBLE SAYS ABOUT RUSSIA, ISIS, IRAN, AND THE END TIMES

CHARLES DYER AND MARK TOBEY

NELSON
BOOKS

An Imprint of Thomas Nelson

Published in Nashville, Tennessee, by Nelson Books, an imprint of Thomas Nelson. Nelson Books and Thomas Nelson are registered trademarks of HarperCollins Christian Publishing, Inc.

Thomas Nelson titles may be purchased in bulk for educational, business, fundraising, or sales promotional use. For information, please e-mail SpecialMarkets@ ThomasNelson.com.

Any Internet addresses, phone numbers, or company or product information printed in this book are offered as a resource and are not intended in any way to be or to imply an endorsement by Thomas Nelson, nor does Thomas Nelson vouch for the existence, content, or services of these sites, phone numbers, companies, or products beyond the life of this book.

Unless otherwise noted, Scripture quotations are taken from the Holy Bible, New International Version®, NIV®. Copyright © 1973, 1978, 1984, 2011 by Biblica, Inc.™ Used by permission of Zondervan. All rights reserved worldwide. www.zondervan.com

Scripture quotations marked NKJV are from the New King James Version. © 1982 by Thomas Nelson, Inc. Used by permission. All rights reserved.

Scripture quotations marked NLT are from the *Holy Bible*, New Living Translation. © 1996. Used by permission of Tyndale House Publishers, Inc., Wheaton, Illinois 60189. All rights reserved.

ISBN 978–0–718089726 (eBook)

Library of Congress Cataloging-in-Publication Data

Names: Dyer, Charles H., 1952-author. | Tobey, Mark (Mark T.), author.
Title: Clash of kingdoms: what the Bible says about Russia, ISIS, Iran, and the end times / Charles Dyer and Mark Tobey.
Description: Nashville, Tennessee: Nelson Books, [2017] | Includes bibliographical references.
Identifiers: LCCN 2016036964 | ISBN 9780718089597
Subjects: LCSH: Bible—Prophecies. | Eschatology. | End of the world. | World politics—21st century—Forecasting.
Classification: LCC BS647.3 .D94 2017 | DDC 220.^{1}/5—dc23 LC record available at https://lccn.loc.gov/2016036964

Printed in the United States of America

17 18 19 20 21   LSC   10 9 8 7 6 5 4 3 2 1

For our dads . . .
Charles W. Dyer and Thomas G. Tobey, for their
example of hard work and for instilling in us the serious
importance of lifelong education and scholarship . . .
and for the sacrifices they made for us and for our
families over all these years. We are indebted to them.

CONTENTS

CONTENTS

FOREWORD

Scan your local paper, watch the evening news, or go online and read the headlines at Google News. Whether the focus is on local, national, or international events, nearly every story quickly descends into scenes of unsolvable chaos. Hopelessness and fear seem to grip so much of the world. And even seasoned followers of Jesus can grow bewildered and depressed.

Part of the reason I wrote *Is This the End?* was to help believers maintain their spiritual footing while navigating the moral quicksand of our world. As I wrote, I searched for historically accurate as well as biblically relevant sources to supplement my own study. One resource I found particularly helpful was *The ISIS Crisis*, written by Charles Dyer and Mark Tobey. What drew me to their writing was their ability to synthesize current events while retaining a clear biblical focus and a calm, pastoral perspective.

That's why I also appreciate their latest work, *Clash of Kingdoms*. In this follow-up volume Dyer and Tobey resume where *The ISIS Crisis* left off. While the specter of ISIS continues to haunt our world, *Clash of Kingdoms* sees beyond to larger threats looming just over the horizon. Russia. Iran. A fragmented Europe. And at the very center of the bull's-eye—Israel. Using the same mix of history, current events, and biblical insight the authors assemble the puzzle pieces of our jumbled global culture to show how they fit into the prophetic picture found in God's Word.

If you want to know what rises out of ISIS, read *Clash of Kingdoms* by Charles Dyer and Mark Tobey. Trust me on this: You'll be glad you did.

Dr. David Jeremiah
Senior Pastor, Shadow Mountain
Community Church
Founder, Turning Point

INTRODUCTION

Look Around and Be Wise

Be very careful, then, how you live—not as
unwise but as wise, making the most of every
opportunity, because the days are evil.
—EPHESIANS 5:15–16

LONDON, ENGLAND—In a national referendum the United
Kingdom votes to leave the European Union, sending shock
waves reverberating across the continent and around the world.[1]

NICE, FRANCE—A jihadist delivery truck driver from Tunisia
mows down eighty-four pedestrians during a mile-long rampage.[2]

ANKARA, TURKEY—Following a failed coup attempt, the
government of President Recep Tayyip Erdoğan arrests thousands of soldiers and dismisses nearly three thousand judges

in a purge likely to push Turkey further away from its secular moorings.[3]

Moscow, Russia—The United States and Russia announce agreement on steps to end the five-year civil war in Syria but refuse to elaborate on specific details.[4] The Pentagon expresses skepticism over whether the Russians can be trusted.[5]

Two details underscore the frightening reality behind these four headlines. First, all occurred in just over a three-week period. And second, few grasped the subtle but significant interconnectivity between the different stories. As the world becomes ever more complex and interdependent—and as the rate of global change accelerates—our ability to sort through all the data to discover those points of connectivity diminishes. We might try to keep up with *what* is happening in the world, but we do so at the expense of understanding *why*.

Topics shift and jolt from one to the next at mind-boggling rates. And as a result, we find ourselves battered by fear, anxiety, resentment, and even rage—all the while struggling to grasp the significance of one world-changing event even as another pushes it aside to take its place.

Networks, bloggers, and pundits struggle to get the jump on the competition, all vying for the public's coveted attention.

Over the past decade the United States has experienced shockingly diminished respect for its reputation around the world. The Middle East lies in tatters while ISIS continues to fan the flames of religious hatred across the region, leaving Syria, Iraq, and Libya smoldering in its wake.

Israel shudders in utter disbelief as its once staunch and reliable ally, the United States, lifts virtually all sanctions from the terrorist-sponsoring Iranians, offering to them the deal of the century. The result is a globe-sized leadership vacuum that Vladimir Putin, president of Russia, has been all too happy to fill. Posters of Putin are popping up on cars and billboards in parts of Syria and Iraq, praising the Russian military intervention in Syria.[6]

As the Middle East continues to burn, a refugee crisis in Europe is straining the continent's political and economic vitality to the near breaking point. Tens of thousands of men, women, and children—mostly Syrian refugees—languish in makeshift holding camps across Europe as well as in Turkey, Jordan, and Lebanon.

WHAT JUST HAPPENED?

If you've picked up this book, you've likely done so because you're wondering what in the world it all means. You're not alone. Many others have the same questions. But here's some encouragement: if you are attempting to understand what's happening, you're actually fulfilling a part of God's will for you—that you work to understand the times in which we live and be deliberate about redeeming them for good.

There's no question that it would be easy to sit and wring

our hands while witnessing all the chaos, perhaps even to wonder if the end is near.

Thankfully, we are not left to ourselves to try to figure everything out. We have been given a clear and calm guide to world events and all things future to help us find our way.

That guide is the Bible—and in particular, the grand passages of prophecy—which provides real perspective and clarity amid the tumultuous and remarkable sequence of world events that cause our collective heads to spin. The apostle Peter reminds us of this reality:

> We also have the prophetic message as something completely reliable, and you will do well to pay attention to it, as to a light shining in a dark place, until the day dawns and the morning star rises in your hearts. (2 Peter 1:19)

Both of us, Mark and Charlie, have discovered firsthand how this message, properly understood, can help believers remain calm amid the chaos.

THE POWER AND PERSPECTIVE OF PROPHECY

Mark's Story

One particular autumn when Mark was serving as a pastor, he was teaching on the subject of prophecy during the Wednesday evening prayer meetings. Given the rise of interest in all things Middle East, he had decided to offer a brief five-week session on what the Bible teaches about current events. Mark asked his young staff to arrange an extra row of fifteen chairs, just in case there was interest beyond the typical Wednesday evening crowd.

The church office sent out a congregation-wide e-mail announcing the new Wednesday night topic, and they ran a small print ad in the Sunday bulletin the week before the start. Mark also made one extra pot of coffee—just in case!

The meeting usually began around 6:30 p.m. By 6:15 the place was packed and staff were scrambling to set up additional chairs. Eventually they had to arrange seating in an adjacent foyer and run sound into that makeshift overflow. The response and interest never dropped off the entire five weeks!

In fact, week after week, people came up afterward to ask, "Don't you think we're getting close to the end?" Or, "Based on all these passages, wouldn't you agree the Lord's coming could be soon?"

The highlight of those five weeks, though, came on an evening when Mark was teaching through Paul's explanation of the Lord's return in 1 Thessalonians 5. Paul wrote to the Thessalonian believers:

> Now, brothers and sisters, about times and dates we do not
> need to write to you, for you know very well that the day of
> the Lord will come like a thief in the night. (vv. 1–2)

Mark emphasized how Paul urged the believers at Thessalonica to be alert and vigilant, and not to be caught unprepared spiritually for Christ's return. There was no time like the present, in light of all that was happening in the world, to get right and stay right with the Lord.

Afterward, a young single mother came up to the podium and asked to speak to Mark. She confessed the lesson had spoken directly to her and that the preceding lessons on these prophetic passages had put in her a state of unease about her own spiritual condition. She asked if Mark would help her understand how to find a relationship with God. They bowed together in prayer as she opened her heart to the Savior.

That night was a reminder that God gave these great prophecies not to alarm us, but to prepare us so that we would remain calm and active when unusual or catastrophic events occur. In short, He gave us prophecy to cultivate our spiritual readiness.

Charlie's Story

Charlie was also teaching through 1 and 2 Thessalonians in a Sunday evening series at his church. Attendance was strong and interest was high, especially as the group explored Paul's description of future events. People were eager to understand the prophetic message of these two books of the Bible.

Charlie's aha moment came while teaching through 2 Thessalonians 2. That's where Paul warned the followers of Christ in the church "not to become easily unsettled or alarmed by the teaching allegedly from us—whether by a prophecy or by word of mouth or by letter—asserting that the day of the Lord has already come" (v. 2). Even in the earliest days of the church, there were false reports trying to connect current events to the second coming of Jesus.

But Charlie's moment of clarity wasn't the realization that fears about the future were part of the church's DNA from the very beginning. What really stood out to Charlie was how Paul addressed the problem. Paul first rehearsed for his audience the basics of Bible prophecy—focusing especially on key points from the prophet Daniel and from Jesus. And then he added, "Don't you remember that when I was with you I used to tell you these things?" (v. 5).

Paul had spent only a short time in Thessalonica (Acts 17:1–9), and yet he had taught the Thessalonians what the Bible had to say about the future. More than that, he expected them to call to mind what he had taught so they could keep from becoming "unsettled or alarmed." Acquiring God's perspective on the future has a way of keeping His people properly centered and focused.

Charlie visualized this truth by displaying photographs of book covers from recent works that had sensationalized Bible prophecy, setting specific dates or presenting obscure signs that supposedly reveal end-time events. The difficult part of planning the lesson was deciding which book covers to use. There were too many examples from which to choose! Sensationalism sells—at least until the predicted date or event has passed. Then the initial feeling of foreboding, excitement, or zeal is replaced with disappointment, disillusion, disaffection, and distrust of prophecy in general.

But don't worry! The next world crisis will generate still another blockbuster bestseller!

THE BIBLE AND THE HEADLINES

Such fascination surrounding end-times prophecy has increased exponentially in the last half century—and there seems to be nothing to alter that trajectory. Unfortunately many people, including Christians, end up being shaken emotionally and spiritually when world events unfold in unexpected and dramatic ways and the clash of kingdoms and nations intensifies before their eyes.

Take, for instance, the rise of the young senator from Chicago, Barack Obama, who quickly catapulted from relative obscurity to the presidency of the United States. Some devout Christians were certain he was the Antichrist because of the ease with which he spoke and how quickly he garnered accolades from rulers and nations around the world.[7] Such an overreaching conclusion and irrational response revealed a fundamental problem in how many use prophecy: it's difficult—and dangerous—to try to match bits and pieces of current world events with God's prophetic program because we don't possess His eternal perspective.

But God has provided a better way.

WHEN THE WORLD EXPLODES

Imagine what it would have been like to be in Abraham's sandals when he heard God say, "Go from your country, your people and your father's household to the land I will show you" (Gen. 12:1).

That's exactly what Abraham did. He journeyed from southern Iraq to the land of Canaan, accompanied by his entire family, a host of servants and hired hands, and numerous livestock and herds. And along the way he struggled with famine, he dealt with family problems, and he even fought off foreign invaders. But the greatest threat of all must have been the events described in Genesis 18–19. Abraham witnessed one of the most dramatic and explosive events in all history—the sudden, complete destruction of two of the most significant cities in the Middle East, Sodom and Gomorrah. The heavens opened, and fire and brimstone rained down on these and other nearby towns, wiping out the entire population.

Imagine that happening today. Imagine the breaking news coverage on every channel—the havoc and chaos and confusion that would ensue. Just think of the fear such an event could bring on people. What would you say to your children? What would you ask the Lord? Imagine how your faith would be shaken, how fear would threaten to overwhelm your mind and emotions, and how the level of alarm would rise in your children's minds.

Yet, before God brought judgment on Sodom and Gomorrah, He prepared Abraham for what was about to occur.

> "Shall I hide from Abraham what I am about to do? Abraham will surely become a great and powerful nation, and all nations on earth will be blessed through him. . . ." Then the LORD said, "The outcry against Sodom and Gomorrah is so great and their sin so grievous that I will go down and see if what they have done is as bad as the outcry that has reached me. If not, I will know." (Gen. 18:17–21)

What followed was a back-and-forth negotiation between God and Abraham for the welfare of a few faithful people in those doomed cities.

Ultimately, God judged these cities for their sins, and they were utterly destroyed. Yet Abraham's faith was not shaken—it was bolstered. Why? Because God had revealed His plan beforehand. Abraham could pass through that time of calamity with a peace and readiness he would otherwise not have known.

That's the power of prophecy. Knowing what the Bible says about the future can help us put current events in their proper perspective. God reveals His plans and purposes to us not so we will shrink in fear but so we will continue to walk and live by faith.

WHERE WE GO FROM HERE

In *Clash of Kingdoms* we hope to demonstrate both the power and the perspective of the Bible as it relates to the often confusing and unsettling circumstances surrounding current events. Can we make sense of everything unfolding today? Is God setting the stage for an ultimate world conflict? Will ISIS play a part? What does Russia really want? How do other nations fit into God's overall program? And to what extent does the Bible unveil God's program for the future?

In the coming pages, we'll look at ISIS and how this bloodthirsty terrorist state continues to ravage the Middle East and encroach upon the world's sense of security and calm. We'll explore Russia and what may be behind its reemergence onto the world scene. We'll also examine Iran, Iraq, and Syria to see how the chaos in these countries is reshaping the contours of this ancient and strife-weary region. We'll investigate the apparent disintegration of the European Union as a unified and compelling entity on the world stage to see how it might be able to refashion itself into a new Western order as part of God's end-times drama. And we'll focus on Israel, a small nation with a starring role in God's future plans for this planet.

As you begin this book, you may be experiencing one of two reactions. The first is apathy—why does any of it matter? *Since I can't do anything about what's happening in the rest of the world, why bother? I'll just go on living my life.* The other reaction you might be experiencing is anxiety—feeling as if the darkness and chaos of evil forces beyond your control are threatening you and everyone you love. If you're feeling either of these two very powerful emotions, we point you once again to the words of the apostle Paul, who exclaimed,

> *Awake, you who sleep,*
> *Arise from the dead,*
> *And Christ will give you light.* (Eph. 5:14 NKJV)

ONE

THE PROBLEM OF NATIONS

Nation will rise against nation, and kingdom
against kingdom. There will be famines
and earthquakes in various places.
—MATTHEW 24:7

In the preface to his book *A Durable Peace: Israel and Its Place Among the Nations*, Benjamin Netanyahu, Israel's prime minister, tells a compelling story that highlights Israel's enigmatic significance:

> During the Gulf War, Israel sustained thirty-nine Scud missile attacks that rained down on its cities. Deafening sirens warned Israelis to don their gas masks in the tense minutes as the missiles headed for their targets. In the course of one such alert I was being interviewed, with a gas mask on, at the CNN television headquarters in Jerusalem.

After the alert subsided, the CNN bureau chief, evidently moved by the experience, asked me to show the network's viewers Israel's position on the map of the Middle East.

"Show them what you showed me in your office the other day," he said, producing a map of the Middle East in front of the camera.

"Here's the Arab world," I said, "walking" across the map with my hands open wide. It took me a number of handbreadths to span the twenty-one Arab countries.

"And here is Israel," I added, easily covering it with my thumb.[1]

Israel might indeed be small geographically. But never confuse size with significance. This small nation has played a very large role in human history. And, as Jesus shared with His disciples, that starring role will continue into the future.

ALL ABOUT ISRAEL

The sun sank begrudgingly behind the western horizon as Jesus, accompanied by His ministry-weary disciples, exited the temple court. Trudging through the Kidron Valley, now draped in shadows, Jesus and His followers began the steep walk up the Mount of Olives. Midway up the slope they once again felt the afternoon sun on their backs. Turning around, they paused a moment to allow their eyes to adjust to the sudden brightness.

As the sun reflected off the limestone and marble buildings, the disciples marveled at the splendor of Herod's temple. Imagine their shock at Jesus' blunt announcement of its impending destruction:

> "Truly I tell you, not one stone here will be left on another; every one will be thrown down." (Matt. 24:2)

Jesus' words left the Twelve stunned and confused. Each in his own way labored to line up the events and struggles of living in first-century Judea, always in fear of Rome's iron-clad hold over their homeland and way of life, with a limited knowledge of the prophets' oracles and the already-ancient promise to Abraham to establish Israel as a nation forever.

Would God be faithful to Israel as He had promised to Abraham centuries before? What about Rome and the other Gentile nations bordering the land of promise? How would those people fit into God's program and plan? As Rome intensified its persecution and intolerance of all who dared to disobey, would following Jesus bring little more than death to all who aligned themselves with Him?

Jesus sat down comfortably under the branches of one of the many olive trees nestled peacefully on this mountain just to the east of Jerusalem and answered:

> "Watch out that no one deceives you. For many will come in my name, claiming, 'I am the Messiah,' and will deceive many. You will hear of wars and rumors of wars, but see

to it that you are not alarmed. Such things must happen, but the end is still to come. Nation will rise against nation, and kingdom against kingdom. There will be famines and earthquakes in various places. All these are the beginning of birth pains." (Matt. 24:4–8)

The words Jesus spoke to His disciples could also be addressed to His followers today. Only moments into any television news broadcast or Internet news stream, we are confronted with reports of another frightening terrorist attack, or a bold and bizarre military move by Russia, or a ballistic test missile from Iran. The news spills into our family rooms and penetrates our collective conscience.

Local and national news is just as unsettling. Reports on the rapid shift in long-held beliefs—from personal morality to marriage and family values—blast from the television or computer at an ever-alarming rate. And these are followed by reports of a crumbling health-care system; spiraling costs; previously unknown dangers, such as the Zika virus; and any number of other strange and frightening health-care risks lurking in the shadows.

All these news stories bring a chilling unease to anyone even remotely aware of how quickly and completely the world seems to have closed in around us. North Korea, once safely on the other side of the world, now threatens to annihilate millions of Americans on the West Coast. As Greece's economy teetered on the brink of total collapse, everyone wondered just how vulnerable other nations might be. Could the collapse of one country bring economic disaster to others? And then the eyes of the world turned to Europe as the Brexit crisis dramatically altered the political, economic, and social landscape of an entire continent.

As the world becomes smaller and even more interconnected, our questions echo the queries of the followers of Jesus on that hillside overlooking the temple:

> "When will this happen, and what will be the sign of your coming?" (Matt. 24:3)

AN ALIGNMENT OF NATIONS

Before God selected Abraham as an intermediary, He had been revealing Himself directly to all humanity. But the rebellion at Babel and the scattering of the nations required a new approach. God needed someone through whom He could reach out and bless the scattered nations. The one He chose was Abraham, originally called Abram. When God called Abraham, He said:

> *"I will bless those who bless you,*
> *and whoever curses you I will curse;*
> *and all peoples on earth*
> *will be blessed through you."* (Gen. 12:3)

Beginning with Abraham God revealed a plan, purpose, and destiny for his descendants and for the Gentiles. The two intersected in a land later called Israel.

With few natural resources and marginal rainfall, some might wonder why this tiny landmass, linking three continents, has occupied such a central place in world history. Why does Israel always seem to be at the center of the world's attention—and the object of such conflicting passions?

Somewhere among the Bible's ancient prophecies and the complex geopolitical and global intricacies of our modern world is the secret to how everything will unfold. To be sure, Israel will be at the center, and all the other nations of the world will either "bless" her—and in turn be blessed—or "curse" her and conspire to bring about her destruction, to their own peril.

To understand current events in light of the Bible, we must first embrace a singular and overarching principle of interpretation: the principle of *God and kingdoms*. From the opening refrain of Genesis to the glorious benediction of John's Revelation, the biblical story begins and ends with the *clash of kingdoms*—the epic struggle of righteous and unrighteous kingdoms, those who serve and honor the God of the Bible and those who refuse to bow the knee to His name.

UNDERSTANDING KINGDOMS

The Bible portrays all world events—past, present, and future—within the context of kingdoms and nations. From the very beginning God has ordained the unfolding of time through human agents—rulers, overseers, and kings.

Take, for instance, how the entire story of humanity begins. Once God created the heavens and the earth, fanned out the universe, and set in place all things, He then created the first man and woman, as told to us in Genesis 1:26:

> Then God said, "Let us make mankind in our image, in our likeness, so that they may rule over the fish in the sea and the birds in the sky, over the livestock and all the wild animals, and over all the creatures that move along the ground."

God later issued a strong and exhilarating command to Adam, the first human:

> "Be fruitful and increase in number; fill the earth and subdue it. Rule over the fish in the sea and the birds in the sky and over every living creature that moves on the ground." (v. 28)

Inherent in God's design and purpose for humanity was His desire that we rule the world around us—governing and superintending all God had created. God did not intend for us to rule in a selfish, it's-all-mine-and-I-can-do-what-I-want way. Rather, He intended for humanity to nurture, tend, supervise, and develop His creation. Our God-given role was to cultivate and take care of His creation (Gen. 2:15).

Something went horribly wrong, however, highlighting yet another kingdom reality—the kingdom of darkness, ruled by God's enemy, the Devil. God set His creation in order, and Satan immediately began his devastating venture to undermine God's righteous rule in the earth by deceiving God's highest creation—humanity.

The entry of sin's dark shadow on the human experience set in motion both a cosmic and an earthly battle of kingdoms. On the one side are God and those who by faith have aligned themselves with Him, while on the other side are those who, through ignorance or outright defiance, "stand around with sinners, or join in with mockers" (Ps. 1:1 NLT).

David, Israel's shepherd-king, wrote about this conflict of kingdoms:

> *Why do the nations conspire*
> *and the peoples plot in vain?*
> *The kings of the earth rise up*
> *and the rulers band together*
> *against the LORD and against his anointed.* (Ps. 2:1–2)

The nations of the earth not only rage against each other: they rage against the righteous rule of God.

Virtually every news cycle reports yet another skirmish between warring factions somewhere in the world. Presidents versus prime ministers, dictators versus democracies, or ruling elite versus populous insurgencies—all share in common the complicated global, socioeconomic, and geopolitical minefield that has come to define our fractured and fragile global culture.

THE CONNECTED WORLD

When Jesus spoke of nations rising against nations in Matthew 24, He had a very specific period of time in mind—that period of time just before His return to earth. The events of that time reach their climax in verse 30 when "all the peoples of the earth" see the "Son of Man coming on the clouds of heaven, with power and great glory." But in another sense His words also can apply to a day like ours, when a global economy, aided by satellite and Internet technology and the dissemination of real-time information at lightning speed, can contribute to global conflict. We live in a shrinking world where the threat of an economic collapse in Greece or a vote in the United Kingdom to leave the European Union can send a financial tsunami across the entire global marketplace.

But the world's interconnectedness extends beyond the financial markets.

A viral outbreak in a remote village in Asia, Africa, or South America can now set the entire world on edge—scrambling to develop vaccines and other protective measures—because air travel and porous international borders have accelerated the speed at which such viruses can spread. Being part of a connected world has generated unintended consequences.

When immense numbers of Muslim refugees from Syria flooded into Greece and then into the rest of Europe, nations already facing economic and social pressures began to buckle under the strain, generating a voter backlash that has threatened to topple governments. "Brexit is just the 'tip of the iceberg' of popular resentment against the EU that could destroy the entire bloc, economists have warned."[2]

Nations are connected to nations—and Jesus said they will rise against each other in the end times.

Economies are connected. Cultures and systems intersect, collide, and absorb each impact as the world responds to ever-increasing social, economic, political, and ideological upheaval.

The words of Jesus sound eerily relevant when He declared to His bewildered disciples, "This is only the first of the birth pains, with more to come" (Matt. 24:8 NLT). As we sense the tension in the nations around the world, we wonder if the birth pains have started.

It all has to do with "the nations."

GOD'S TWOFOLD DIVISION OF NATIONS

Most of the Old Testament centers around God revealing Himself to Israel. Yet there is also much that is revealed about the significance of the other nations of the world—the Gentiles. Understanding the relationships among the various nations mentioned in the Scriptures is key to making sense of world events today, especially as those events point toward a pre-determined end-time conflict. And the central focus of this final conflict will be the land God promised to the nation Israel.

"Nations in the Word of God are divided on the basis of their relationship to the nation of Israel," wrote the late Dr. J. Dwight Pentecost, biblical scholar and expert on end-times prophecy.[3] Pentecost and others like him believe the ultimate world conflict between nations will happen when world powers align against the nation of Israel in a cataclysmic world event, as predicted in the Bible. But why so much to-do about Israel, such a seemingly geographically insignificant piece of real estate?

A message repeated throughout the Hebrew Scriptures is that God will bless any nation that supports and defends Israel, while any nation seeking to harm or destroy Israel will pay a heavy price.

But what events could lead nations to take such drastic measures? Why, among all the nations of the world, does Israel draw such consistently unfriendly fire? How can we, as followers of God and students of His Word, view and understand current events in such a way as to not panic and recoil but rather be compelling in our testimonies of faith—and unwavering in our support for Israel?

These questions deserve to be answered as we wind through the convoluted maze of media reports and real-time descriptions of warring nations, economic uncertainties, and Bible prophecies.

Is there a power in the world today that will begin to bring the enemies of Israel together? Will such forces and fractures, now intensifying, erupt unexpectedly? Or will they gradually build over decades? Is there one single nation that will ultimately rise up and ignite the flame of conflict?

As the world focuses its attention and resources on the insidious and violent metastasizing of ISIS, perhaps a more sinister threat silently lurks just out of sight, preparing the weapons it intends to unleash upon a polarized and distracted world.

TWO

THE BEAR IS BACK

What About Russia?

You will come from your place in the far north,
you and many nations with you, all of them riding
on horses, a great horde, a mighty army.
—EZEKIEL 38:15

In 1986, author Tom Clancy wrote a frighteningly realistic novel titled *Red Storm Rising*, a fictional tale built on a provocative premise. Facing economic collapse, the Soviet Union embarks on a bold move to seize the oil fields of the Middle East in order to survive economically.

More than thirty years later, could life be imitating art?

Red Storm Rising depicts the Soviet Union's attempt to overcome NATO by launching a series of conventional attacks coupled with orchestrated acts of deception. The story begins in 1980 at a very productive, but old, Soviet oil refinery in Nizhnevartovsk. The refinery is blown up by Islamic terrorists, and the devastation takes the Soviet Union to the brink of economic collapse through a sudden drop in its supply of refined petroleum. Though the novel focuses on the unfolding events in Europe and the North Atlantic, the Soviet Union's ultimate objective in the novel is to intimidate the West into inaction so their forces can push south against the Arab states and gain control over their oil fields and refineries.

Clancy's fictional tale links national rivalries, geography, oil, and religion in ways that are eerily similar to current events. It's not a terrorist attack on a strategic oil refinery that threatens the economic viability of Russia today, but rather an oil glut that has resulted in a dramatic slide in the price of oil.

The economic sanctions imposed on Russia by the United States, Europe, and Japan for its aggressive actions against Ukraine have taken an enormously heavy toll on Russia's economy. These sanctions have also offended the collective soul of the Russian people, and Vladimir Putin has used this perceived threat to rally Russians behind his aggressive plans to restore his country's greatness.

Eager to win back world prominence and driven perhaps by his own more insidious motives, the Russian leader has shown no hesitation in continuing his threats against Eastern Europe and in extending Russia's influence across the Middle East.

Not since the Russian invasion of Afghanistan in the late 1970s and early 1980s have the Russians shown such penetrating interest and military involvement in the Middle East.

Sucked into a disastrous nine-year battle against Islamic extremists in Afghanistan, the Soviet Union hobbled through a costly and politically damaging war until eventually pulling out in embarrassment and defeat.

Fast-forward three decades and Russia is back in the news, sending troops into Syria to support President Bashar al-Assad. Though paying lip service to the aim of halting the advance of ISIS forces in the region, these troops were really sent to help Assad fight off rebel forces attempting to topple his cruel and corrupt regime.

Putin and Russia's involvement in the war-torn country of Syria has been driven by several significant priorities. Their primary goal is to secure the long-term stability of Assad's government in Syria, thereby cementing Russia's own interests in that country.

Second, the conflict has provided a bold demonstration of Russia's increasingly modernized armed forces and high-tech weaponry. And thanks to a nonstop media cycle, the entire world has been watching. Syria has become a combination proving ground and dealer showroom for the Russian arms industry.

Third, Putin has had a strong interest in stemming the tide of Islamic extremism in the region. Russia has had an ongoing struggle with jihadist fighters from Chechnya and the Caucasus regions. Thousands of fighters from this area have aligned themselves with ISIS. Better to fight against ISIS in Syria than to have these jihadists return and continue their fight inside the Russian Federation.

But most ominously, Russia sees an opportunity to expand its influence in the Middle East. As the United States pulls back from its historic role as the leader in the Middle East, Russia appears willing to invest its resources in the region—to become the new power broker in the deadly game of thrones unfolding there.

The rapidly shifting landscape of alliances and allies have upended a hundred years of assumed reality across the Middle East. Furthermore, Russia appears eager to shape this new reality to suit its own ends. It's now possible to envision a framework by which Putin or a successor might cobble together a coalition of otherwise dissimilar states in a new alliance. But what could unite the different ethnic and religious factions?

Perhaps a common goal—or a common enemy. And the one common enemy for many countries in that region of the world is Israel. Could Russia build a coalition united in their desire to move against Israel?

RUSSIA IN THE BIBLE

Most Bible students with even cursory understanding of biblical prophecy suspect that Russia will play some strategic role in end-time events. Once considered by many Americans the epitome of evil during the days of the Soviet Union and the Cold War, Russia experienced something of a rehabilitation in the minds and hearts of Christians after the fall of the Iron Curtain. During the past three decades, many Christians from the United States and Europe traveled to Russia to help establish mission efforts there. Armed with the gospel and a deep burden for the hearts and souls of its people, Christians sought to bring healing to a region marked by generations of Communist rule and atheist indoctrination.

As the Communist hammer and sickle was replaced by the red, white, and blue flag of modern Russia, people mostly stopped assuming Ezekiel's prophecy was about Russia. But history now seems to be repeating itself with the breathtaking energy of a Tom Clancy novel.

As current events grow increasingly more aligned with the Bible's never-changing prophecies, an ultimate battle of kingdoms once again comes more clearly into view. World events and the conflicts between kingdoms seem to be aligning and pointing toward that time of final conflagration.

PUTIN'S WORLD

Vladimir Putin shows little restraint in canvassing the globe in search of willing allies. He desires nothing short of the glory, vibrancy, and international influence once possessed by his beloved Russia. He seeks to throw off the decades of economic and political marginalization that made life so intolerable for her millions of citizens. Russia's conflicts with Georgia (in 2008) and Ukraine (since 2014) suggest Putin's goal is the rebuilding of the empire that fell along with the Berlin Wall.

But where would Putin, the political chess master, make his next move?

The answer came in 2015 with the arrival of Russian troops and aircraft in Syria. The perpetual instability of the Middle East and the ever-elusive dream of peace between Israel and her neighbors continue to fan the flames of unrest in this increasingly unstable part of the world. But chaos can be fertile soil for someone seeking new ways to grow an empire.

For decades, world leaders have found it nearly impossible to reach a peaceful resolution to all the conflicts in the Middle East. Instead, the region has continually erupted in firestorms of confusion and violence. ISIS and other Islamic extremists are simply the most recent example of the different dictators and despots who have tried to step into the leadership vacuum.

The Bible predicts there will be a force—a world power—that will successfully unite all the disparate allies against a common foe—Israel.

Ezekiel 38 paints a detailed portrayal of an array of nations that join forces ultimately to attack Israel at a time when the country will be experiencing a rare time of peace:

> The word of the LORD came to me: "Son of man, set your face against Gog, of the land of Magog, the chief prince of Meshek and Tubal; prophesy against him and say: 'This is what the Sovereign LORD says: I am against you, Gog, chief prince of Meshek and Tubal. I will turn you around, put hooks in your jaws and bring you out with your whole

army—your horses, your horsemen fully armed, and a great horde with large and small shields, all of them brandishing their swords. Persia, Cush and Put will be with them, all with shields and helmets, also Gomer with all its troops, and Beth Togarmah from the far north with all its troops— the many nations with you.'" (vv. 1–6)

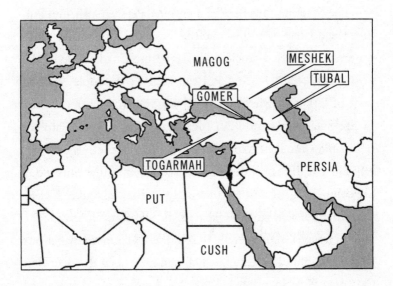

These nations identified by the prophet might not be listed on any modern map, but they existed as vibrant entities in Ezekiel's day. This map shows where Magog, Meshek, Tubal, Persia, Cush, Put, Gomer, and Beth Togarmah were located.

The leader of this coalition of nations is identified by Ezekiel as a man named Gog who is from the land of Magog. This future leader emerges as a ruthless, forceful commander who sets his mind on overtaking and overwhelming by force any opposing nation. He possesses a bold and shocking hubris that defies the world leaders of his day. The land he rules, Magog, has been identified by some scholars as the region north of the Black Sea, the area we know today as Russia and Ukraine. In Ezekiel 38:3, the prophet also mentions both Meshek and Tubal, which today occupy the Caucasus region that straddles the borders of Russia, Turkey, and Iran.

The other nations Ezekiel mentions, Persia, Cush, and Put, join the coalition led by this leader named Gog. On a modern map, the area of ancient Persia is Iran. Cush would be the area south of Egypt, and Put represents the people residing west of Egypt in what is now Libya. The final nations listed by Ezekiel, Gomer and Beth Togarmah, were on the Anatolian peninsula—modern Armenia and Turkey, respectively.

The parallels between Ezekiel's prophecy and events today are compelling, almost frighteningly so. Ezekiel makes it clear that this coalition will assemble in "future years" to invade the land of Israel, "whose people were gathered from many nations to the mountains of Israel, which had long been desolate" but that now "live in safety" (Ezek. 38:8). From the day Ezekiel penned those words until the reestablishment of the modern state of Israel, his prediction wasn't capable of being fulfilled. It's only been in the last four or five decades that Israel has experienced a relative sense of safety as a nation.

Ezekiel identified the leader of the invading coalition as a man ruling over Meshek and Tubal, the Caucausus region between the Black and Caspian Seas—land controlled, or coveted, by Russia.

Ezekiel compares the future ruler of Magog to a man

named Gog—most likely an allusion to an ancient king named Gyges who died about seventy years before Ezekiel delivered his prophecy. By identifying this still-future ruler as "Gog," Ezekiel was using someone from his recent past to paint a one-word portrait of this future ruler. It is similar to someone today identifying the future Antichrist as the next "Hitler" or "Stalin"—men who also died several decades ago but whose evil legacy is still fresh on people's minds.

Can we be more specific in identifying this ruler named Gog? A short answer is no. Only time will tell who is in view. But it does seem clear that the passage is pointing to the leader of the area now controlled by Russia. And we can see significant parallels between what Ezekiel predicted and what is happening in the Middle East today. Russia and Iran are allies. Russia and Turkey are once again exploring ways to realign their national interests. And most importantly, Israel is again back in the land.

THAT FOX AND THE PURPOSES OF GOD

Not long before Jesus would face crucifixion His disciples warned Him about the dangers of Herod Antipas, a descendant of Herod the Great. Jesus replied:

> "Go tell that fox, 'I will keep on driving out demons and healing people today and tomorrow, and on the third day I will reach my goal.'" (Luke 13:32)

Much like Herod Antipas of Jesus' day, Russia's President Putin seemingly continues to cunningly outfox even the most sophisticated of world leaders in order to feed his insatiable appetite for power, influence, and national popularity. But the Bible makes plain that despite the clever and darkened motives of world leaders such as Putin, it will be the purposes of God that will be accomplished and satisfied according to His perfect, sovereign plan.

Ezekiel's prophecy cracks open a window into how events and movements we are witnessing today could align to become a framework that will be used by a powerful and insidious leader to unite the nations of the world against Israel. The world has fixated so intently on ISIS that it has paid less attention to Russia. But could the battle against ISIS actually be setting the stage for an even greater confrontation between kingdoms?

To answer that, we need to take a closer look at ISIS and where it might be heading.

THREE

AFTER ISIS

The Next Bend Along the Road to Armageddon

For our struggle is not against flesh and blood, but against the rulers, against the authorities, against the powers of this dark world and against the spiritual forces of evil in the heavenly realms.

—EPHESIANS 6:12

Without question, ISIS still looms as a major source of anxiety and fear in the minds of Americans—and of many other people around the world. Despite the most intense efforts on the part of sophisticated governments to destroy this rogue Islamic state, ISIS rages on. In spite of the West's supersized, high-tech military hardware, ISIS continues making inroads into the splintered, war-fractured lands of the Middle East and Africa.

What started almost imperceptibly as a radical offshoot of Al-Qaeda soon began rolling through remote villages across Syria and Iraq. Shaving off shares of the limelight from its more infamous predecessor, ISIS blew onto the world scene as the most formidable and frightening force of terror and violence anyone has ever witnessed. Following the death of Osama bin Laden, ISIS gained prominence and power in the dark and evil world of radical Islamic forces and set out to establish a worldwide Muslim caliphate—or Islamic state— with Abu Bakr al-Baghdadi as the new caliph or ruler.

ISIS remained elusive and enigmatic, making it difficult for US military commanders to devise an effective strategy for engagement. Sending in large-scale Western forces would raise the specter of a new "Crusade"—an incursion of the "Christian West" against Islam. Such an approach is what initially helped groups such as ISIS and Al-Qaeda recruit Muslims to their cause. But to fight ISIS using Muslim-dominated armies, with the West providing logistical and air support, risks igniting deeper sectarian and ethnic conflicts among the already tense and divided landscape across the Middle East.

Major General Michael K. Nagata, the former deputy director for Special Operations for the United States in the Middle East, admitted his frustration with the ISIS conundrum: "We have not defeated the idea. We do not even understand the idea."[1]

When President Barack Obama referred to ISIS as "non-Islamic"[2] and Al-Qaeda as a "jayvee team,"[3] he reflected sentiments that demonstrated how confused the West was about the group. Such faulty perspectives, in part, may have contributed to the West's lack of a clear and compelling strategy to defeat ISIS.

WHAT COMES AFTER ISIS?

A well-worn comedic trope involves a doctor telling a patient, "I have some good news and some bad news." As the routine unfolds, the "good news" isn't really good at all—while the bad news is unbelievably worse.

> **DOCTOR:** I have some good news and some bad news.
> You only have twenty-four hours to live.
> **PATIENT:** What's the good news?
> **DOCTOR:** That is the good news. The bad news is that I
> forgot to call you yesterday.

Well, we have some good news and some bad news about ISIS. Unfortunately, there's nothing humorous about this story. The good news is that ISIS is on the decline. The bad news is that ISIS won't be totally eradicated and could very likely be replaced by something even worse.

After more than two years of struggle, the West has finally discovered a two-pronged strategy that appears to be working against ISIS. It first involves training local forces to do the actual fighting. They are Muslim, which eliminates ISIS's ability to claim they are fighting a holy war against Christian crusaders. The second prong requires outfitting and training these local fighters and supporting them with overwhelming air power. Slowly, village by village, this strategy has allowed the different groups in Iraq and Syria to claw back territory from ISIS. From Palmyra to Fallujah, territory has been snatched out of ISIS's control!

Yet that leads to the bad news.

Sputtering world economies, local and national elections, and a host of other domestic issues have already started pushing the war against ISIS out of the spotlight. Apart from intermittent terrorist attacks in Europe or America, the news media and the public will eventually lose interest in ISIS the way they lost interest in Al-Qaeda. Like its predecessor, ISIS will be pushed off the front page long before they are gone. That could prove to be a deadly mistake.

THE FIREBRAND OF ISLAMIC TERROR

ISIS and Al-Qaeda share many of the same goals, though they strongly disagree on the best means to accomplish them. Furthermore, the leaders of both organizations have strong personal egos that make it impossible for them to reconcile. But it would be a mistake to assume the two groups will never overcome their differences. A unified Sunni jihadist organization could still create terrifying havoc around the world.

But the bad news gets worse. In their drive to defeat ISIS, few in the West are daring to ask a greater question: What will arise to replace ISIS? Assuming ISIS can be forced out of all the territory it now controls in Syria and Iraq, what government will take its place? Most assume Syria and Iraq will return to being unified nation-states, hopefully with more benign democratic governments. But is that realistic?

The fight against ISIS has widened the ethnic and religious chasms in Syria and Iraq. Part of the conflict in both countries centers on the fight for control between Sunnis and Shiites. ISIS and most of the rebel groups in Iraq and Syria are Sunni, while the governments of Iraq and Syria are dominated by Shiites and Alawites, an offshoot of the Shia branch of Islam. If ISIS is defeated, will Sunnis willingly submit to Shiite control? Or have we set the stage for the next round of conflict?

The ethnic divisions in the region add an even greater level of complexity to the puzzle. Both the Kurds and the Turks are Sunnis, but they're *not* Arabs. The Kurds have been very successful at pushing back ISIS, but they have also been highly motivated. They are the fourth largest ethnic group in the Middle East, but they have never been allowed to establish their own independent state. That is something they would like to do, beginning with the land they have liberated from ISIS. But their plans are violently opposed by Turkey, Iran, and those Sunni Arabs in Iraq and Syria who inhabit some of the land liberated by the Kurds.

Remove ISIS from the equation, and the Middle East remains a simmering cauldron of ethnic and religious jealousy and hatred. ISIS capitalized on these divisions to carve out its Sunni-Arab kingdom. No Western-style democracy can successfully eliminate these divisions because they run too deep. Western democratic values such as religious freedom, equal protection under the law, and the rights of minorities clash with Islamic values and Sharia law.

OUTSIDE FORCES

In addition to the religious and ethnic fault lines zigzagging their way across the Middle East, there is one final set of seismic stressors helping to guarantee that chaos will continue long after the demise of ISIS. These are the pressures exerted on the region by four major outside forces—the United States, Russia, Iran, and Turkey. And the shifting dynamic between these forces threatens to expose additional points of tension in an already volatile region.

The United States and Russia have been the dominant outside powers vying for influence in the Middle East for the past half century. The Cold War between the two superpowers extended from the Berlin Wall all the way to the rugged hills of Afghanistan and the rice paddies of Vietnam. In the Middle East, the United States provided military support for Israel, Turkey, and Saudi Arabia, while the Soviet Union initially outfitted Syria, Egypt, and Libya. These alliances began to shift in the 1970s when Anwar Sadat expelled the Soviet military advisers from Egypt and shifted to a growing dependence on the United States. The Soviet withdrawal from Afghanistan, which began in 1988, and the fall of the Berlin

Wall in 1989 signaled an even greater decline within Russia itself. Everything came tumbling down with the dissolution of the Soviet Union in 1991.

As the Soviet Union collapsed, America's power and influence grew. After Saddam Hussein invaded Kuwait, the United States issued an ultimatum and began building a thirty-four-nation coalition to push Iraq out. Led by then president George Herbert Walker Bush, American forces launched their prime-time campaign of Operation Desert Storm, defeating and dislodging the Iraqis in a matter of weeks. For the next decade the United States reigned supreme as the world's sole superpower.

ENTER IRAN

Not everyone was willing to accept America's role as the world's policeman. Al-Qaeda arose, in part, because of the presence of US troops in Saudi Arabia during Operation Desert Storm. The hatred felt by these Sunni extremists toward America was matched by the hatred of the Shiite extremists ruling Iran. After all, Iran had visions of its own greatness. Although only representing about 15 percent of Muslims worldwide, Iran sought to export its brand of Islamic extremism. Its goal was one worthy of the ancient Persian ruler Cyrus—to build a modern Shiite Persian empire that would extend from Iran westward to the Mediterranean. But because of the power and influence of what it calls the "Great Satan" (the United States), Iran had to bide its time.

Iran's opportunity to expand came in the aftermath of the Second Gulf War. Following the attacks on the twin towers of the World Trade Center and the Pentagon, the United States launched a military offensive against Al-Qaeda and put on notice those countries that aided terrorists such as Al-Qaeda and that harbored weapons of mass destruction that could be made available to such groups. America's initial incursion into Afghanistan to oust the Taliban and destroy Al-Qaeda went well, though Osama bin Laden was able to slip away before being captured.

The United States charged Iraq with possessing weapons of mass destruction, and with harboring and supporting terrorist groups such as Al-Qaeda. Although there has been much second-guessing and finger-pointing following the invasion, the reality is that Saddam Hussein had at one time possessed chemical and biological weapons that he used against the Kurds following the first Gulf War. His actual use of such weapons, coupled with his reluctance to cooperate with UN inspectors, gave the impression that he had more such weapons at his disposal.

In March 2003 the United States led a coalition into Iraq to topple Saddam Hussein. Three weeks later Baghdad fell into Allied hands. The battle against the Ba'ath party of Saddam Hussein was over, but the battle for Iraq had just begun. And Iran saw an opportunity to act in the chaos that followed.

In launching its invasion, the United States had been led to believe that most Iraqis hated Saddam Hussein and would welcome the invaders as liberators. But in freeing the country from Hussein, the Allies opened Iraq to sectarian violence. The majority of the population were Shiite, who have a religious affinity for the ayatollahs ruling in Iran. It didn't take long for Iran to encourage the majority Shiites to rise up against the "Crusaders" from the West. The Shiites also sought to turn the tables on the Sunni minority who had for so long dominated the country. America found itself in a quagmire—a national "domestic dispute" in which the two major religious groups fought each other—and both fought the Americans. Iran stoked the violence and helped train and arm the Shiites even as Al-Qaeda found support among the Sunnis.

After the election of President Obama, the United States underwent a change in foreign policy. His promise to bring home America's troops from Iraq and Afghanistan was followed by a promise to pivot away from the Middle East and to focus on the Far East. China, Japan, North and South Korea, and the Philippines became the stated, if not the actual, center of US international diplomacy. A decade-long financial collapse, coupled with a drastic reduction in military spending, caused the United States to pull back and recalibrate its role in the Middle East. The world heard America say it no longer wanted to be the "cop on the beat" in that part of the world.

A door of change had been opened, and Iran hurried to push its way toward the front of those lining up to take America's place.

THE ENIGMA OF TURKEY

The modern country of Turkey rose out of the ashes of the Ottoman Empire. That empire was carved up by Britain and France following World War I. But Mustafa Kemal Atatürk, a Turkish military officer during that war, set out to rebuild his country from those shattered remains. He is credited with founding the modern state of Turkey, which he sought to pattern after the West. The Western Latin alphabet replaced the old Arabic script. Though the vast majority of the people were Muslim, the new nation was designed to be a secular republic. His influence was so pervasive on the formation of the country that the Turkish parliament gave him the surname Atatürk ("father of the Turks") in 1934.

The North Atlantic Treaty Organization (NATO) was born following World War II to help stem the expansion of the Soviet Union. Just three years after its founding, Turkey and Greece were admitted to membership, even though neither country borders the Atlantic Ocean. The expansion made strategic sense at the time because of the fear that the Soviet Union would try to push into the Middle East, disrupting the flow of oil and choking off the transport of goods through the Suez Canal. Turkey was on the front lines against any possible Soviet aggression to the south.

Since the time of Atatürk, Turkey has officially been a secular republic. But at different times elements within the country have tried to push it to the left, toward communism, or to the right, toward Islam. Five times within a thirty-seven-year period, the army staged coups, activating its own "reset button" to restore Turkey to the principles of secular democracy. But in 2007 the army was itself threatened, this time by the European Union. Turkey was trying to join the European Union, a process that involved allowing free and fair elections. A rising Islamist-rooted government won the election and sought to appoint the first-ever Islamist president. The army threatened to intervene, but Europe and the United States objected. If the army were to stage another coup, Europe would view such action as evidence that Turkey was unsuitable for membership in the European Union. The Turkish army was forced to back down.

And ever since that time, Turkey's government has been moving toward political Islam. The short-lived coup attempt in July 2016 revealed the extent to which the military has been muzzled and the power of the Islamist-dominated government has grown.

Turkey's speaker of the parliament, İsmail Kahraman, announced that the principle of secularism "must be removed" from Turkey's constitution. When challenged on the matter, he responded, "As a Muslim country, why should we be in a situation where we are retreating from religion? We are a Muslim country. So we must have a religious constitution."[4]

A secular Turkey aligned with the West has been a political fact of life for the past century. But an Islamic Turkey looking to reengage with the Middle East brings an entirely new set of forces to bear on the region. Will Turkey align with the Sunni Arabs against an Iranian advance? Or will they seek to bridge the divide between Sunni and Shiite and offer a new version of Muslim-dominated democracies working together? Will dreams of a revived Ottoman Empire prove too tempting to resist? One thing is certain: Turkey's future will look vastly different from the original goal stamped into place by Kemal Atatürk.

RUSSIA THE GREAT

"The king is dead! Long live the king!" That phrase was first shouted out in AD 1422 when Charles VII ascended the throne of France following the death of his father. The idea was to announce the new king immediately following the death of the monarch to avoid a possible war of succession. Over time the phrase has taken on a life of its own. (The lira is dead! Long live the euro!) Perhaps the most appropriate use of the phrase during the past two decades applies to the death of the Soviet Union—and the rise of modern Russia.

Few could have imagined in 1991 that today's dominant outside force shaping events in the Middle East would be Russia. But that's exactly what has been happening under Russian president Vladimir Putin.

Putin spent sixteen years as a Soviet KGB agent. He retired from the KGB the year the Soviet Union collapsed and began his meteoric rise in politics, serving multiple terms as either prime minister or president. To understand Russia today, one must understand the mind and heart of Putin. Early in his second term as president, during a nationally televised address to

Russian lawmakers and other top government officials, Putin gave his candid assessment of the collapse of the Soviet Union: "The demise of the Soviet Union was the greatest geopolitical catastrophe of the century."[5]

Putin has worked tirelessly to refashion Russia into a great international power. And the three key pillars on which modern Russia's international policy is built are energy, territorial expansion, and strategic international partnerships. His use of energy to shape the politics of Europe suffered a temporary setback when the global recession and increased exploration led to a worldwide glut in oil and natural gas— and a corresponding collapse in energy prices. Yet Putin hasn't appeared too worried. The law of gravity says that what goes up must come down. The law of supply and demand dictates that what comes down will eventually go back up.

Territorial expansion has proven to be more of a challenge for Putin. In 2008 Russia went to war with Georgia and carved out the so-called states of Abkhazia and South Ossetia. In 2014 Russia invaded and annexed Crimea and supported separatists in eastern Ukraine. And in 2015 Russia sent armed forces into Syria to prop up the faltering government of Bashar al-Assad. The forces sent to Syria changed the course of the conflict, enabling the Syrian government to go on the offensive and reclaim territory that had been lost to ISIS and other rebel forces. But Russia's insertion of forces into the Middle East also raised eyebrows. Some wondered if Putin might be interested in filling the void being left by America's apparent pullback from the region.

Putin's third pillar for rebuilding Russia is based on strategic partnerships. When the United States withheld military hardware from Egypt over its displeasure with the Egyptian army's 2013 overthrow of the Muslim Brotherhood, Russia responded by offering to sell weapons to Egypt. As the relationship between US president Obama and Israeli prime minister Netanyahu began to disintegrate, the one between Putin and Netanyahu grew cozier, with the two leaders meeting three times during a ten-month period.

But the most mystifying partnership in the Middle East is the one formed between Russia and Iran. The relationship developed as the two nations, both under international sanctions, looked for areas of trade where each could benefit from the other. The ties deepened as the two joined to support the Syrian government in its clash with ISIS and the other Sunni rebels. Russia and Iran might support Syria for different reasons, but the battle against ISIS has caused otherwise clashing kingdoms to unite.

Is Russia's interest in the Middle East primarily economic, or are they trying to fill the political void left by the United States? Could Russia's designs on the region be even more sinister?

We'll search out the Bible's answers in the next chapter by looking at one of the Middle East's most prominent players: Iran.

FOUR

DUPLICITOUS IRAN

The Rebuilding of a Persian Power

*I watched the ram as it charged toward the west and
the north and the south. No animal could stand against
it, and none could rescue from its power. It did as it
pleased and became great. . . . The two-horned ram that
you saw represents the kings of Media and Persia.*

—Daniel 8:4, 20

Iran is on the rise.

But the still-unanswered question is what this newly
energized nation hopes to become. Germany's foreign minister
identified Iran as the key to establishing order in the chaotic
Middle East. "We need Iran to calm the conflicts and re-
establish stability in this crisis-hit region. And I hope Iran is
ready for this."[1] His words provide some degree of reassurance,

but unfortunately they aren't being echoed by the leadership of Iran. The lieutenant commander of the Islamic Revolutionary Guards Corps (IRGC) described the relationship between Iran and the West in almost prophetic terms. Echoing Ayatollah Seyed Ali Khamenei's vision of Islam replacing a decaying, dying Western culture, he said:

> While Western civilization is on the wane, an Islamic civilization is rising with a message of freedom, justice, human dignity, restoration of values, true independence, respect for human beings, peace, friendship, calm, security and development for the globe.[2]

So what is happening in Iran, and why does it matter?

Since the overthrow of the shah and the Iranian Revolution under Ayatollah Ruhollah Khomeini in 1979, Iran has experienced nearly four decades of Islamic rule. From the very beginning, the Islamic Republic's relationship with the United States has been mired in conflict. The storming of the US Embassy and the Iran hostage crisis marked the opening salvo. The day after the hostages were seized, Khomeini described the United States as the "Great Satan," a title that continues to be used in Iran's political and religious circles.

Iran endured a catastrophic eight-year war with Iraq that resulted in the deaths of hundreds of thousands of Iranian soldiers and civilians. The damage to Iran's economy was nearly as disastrous. By some estimates the war cost Iran as much as $637 billion.[3] When Ayatollah Khomeini finally accepted the terms of a ceasefire, he declared it to be like drinking from a "poisoned chalice." Perhaps the only element in Iran that benefitted from the war was the Islamic revolution itself. The war strengthened the power of the religious leaders who were able to establish control over every institution within Iran, including the military.

A PESKY PROBLEM

Many Arab countries live in fear of Iran. That fear is based on two cultural differences—religion and ethnicity. Iran, along with southern Iraq, is dominated by Shiite Muslims, while the majority of Muslims in the region are Sunni. As one commentator on the region put it, "The overall Sunni-Shia conflict will play a large role in defining the Middle East as a whole and shaping its relations with the outside world."[4]

But beyond religion, there is also the ethnic conflict between Arabs and Persians. Sadegh Zibakalam, an Iranian intellectual, explained the problem in an interview with *Al Arabiya*: "Iran's attempts to gain supremacy in the region are not triggered by political ambition as much as by a racist drive that pushes Iranians to prove they are superior."[5] This ethnic hatred and distrust is not something recent. It goes back fourteen centuries.

> To many Arabs, the Iranians were arrogant, luxury-loving fire-worshippers and pagans until the Arabs brought them the enlightened message of Islam. To many Iranians, the

Arabs were uncultured nomads who destroyed the great Iranian civilization of the ancient Near East.[6]

From the first days of the Iranian Revolution, the United States imposed heavy economic sanctions on Iran. In January 2002, just four months after 9/11, President Bush identified Iran as one of the three nations in the terrorist "axis of evil." Four years later, the United Nations imposed additional economic sanctions on Iran when it refused to suspend its uranium enrichment program.

In spite of the economic stranglehold, one export from Iran has continued unabated—terrorism. Since 1979 Iran has remained one of the leading promoters of terrorism and terrorist groups worldwide. As recently as June 2016 the US Department of State reported that "Iran remains the leading state sponsor of terrorism globally."[7]

A DEAL WITH THE DEVIL

And yet, in spite of more than thirty years on the State Department's list of terrorist countries, the United States entered into an unprecedented agreement with Iran in which Iran agreed to limit its nuclear program in exchange for the lifting of economic sanctions. The agreement has been applauded and attacked, commended and condemned. Only time will tell which perspective is correct.

What *is* known is that the agreement has several inherent risks. The first is the realization that in exchange for agreeing not to pursue nuclear weapons, Iran has been handed an economic windfall that can be used to support terrorism. Secretary of State John Kerry admitted that some of the money will almost certainly go to terrorist groups. "I think that some of [the money] will end up in the hands of the IRGC [Islamic Revolutionary Guard Corps] or other entities, some of which are labeled terrorists."[8]

A second risk in the nuclear agreement is that it could ultimately destabilize the Middle East. Many of America's traditional allies are concerned by the perceived pivot in America's approach to the Middle East. They see America pulling back from leadership in the region, abandoning its traditional allies, and ceding leadership in the Middle East to Iran. This has Israel, Saudi Arabia, and Egypt searching for new potential partners and suppliers to help them stand against Iran.

Finally, there is a risk that Iran will still develop nuclear weapons. A delay of ten or even fifteen years is a mere tick of the clock from a Middle Eastern perspective. Meanwhile, Iran can continue to perfect its missile technology and design more efficient centrifuges. Did the West buy short-term security by offering Iran a long-term pathway to nuclear weapons? That's the concern. And, of course, even that short-term delay is based on the assumption that Iran won't try to cheat on the agreement.

CLASHING KINGDOMS AND THE
DESIRE OF THE IRANIANS

Could economic prosperity finally change Iran, hopefully making it less bellicose? Can the "beauty" of economic prosperity and the prospects of free and open trade with other nations transform the "beast" of Iran into a civilized prince? It seems that this is the hope of many in the West who want to engage Iran in a way that will smooth out the country's rough edges and round off her sharp theological corners. Is this a wise plan—or nothing more than a fairy tale?

Many responded excitedly when Iran elected "moderates" to parliament. This was seen as a sign that Iran was responding to the nuclear agreement and softening its hard-line perspective on life. Few noticed, however, when the new parliament overwhelmingly reelected an archconservative as its speaker or when the Assembly of Experts selected a hard-line religious leader to oversee the group that will choose the next chief ayatollah to run the country. Like a magician shuffling a deck of cards, everything appears to be in order, but in the end the same card always seems to wind up on top.

Since the founding of the Islamic Republic, Iran has displayed a consistent commitment to two major goals. The first is to support the expansion of militant Islam, especially Shiite Islam. Iran's unflagging support for the Houthis in Yemen, Hezbollah in Lebanon, the Shiite militias in Iraq, and Bashar al-Assad in Syria all share this in common.

Iran's second goal is the destruction of Israel, which they

refer to as the "Zionist entity" and the "little Satan." Iran's Ayatollah Seyed Ali Khamenei expressed it this way:

> The belief that Israel must be eliminated is a condition of our adherence to Islam. . . . Each and every one of our officials should reiterate our responsibility of the need to destroy this cancerous tumor of Israel.[9]

Khamenei did offer a proposal to hold a national referendum within "Palestine" to decide the future of Israel. However, his plan would prohibit most Jews from voting, guaranteeing the state of Israel would be eliminated. But even this nonviolent approach to eliminating Israel is overshadowed by the words written on a long-range missile test-fired by Iran: "Israel must be wiped out."[10]

Iran released a video in August 2015 showing Muslim forces descending on the Dome of the Rock in Jerusalem.[11] They also held well-publicized war games featuring thousands of paramilitary forces from the Revolutionary Guards. The objective of the attack was to seize a large-scale replica of the Dome of the Rock. The exercise was named "Towards the Holy City."[12]

WHEN OPPORTUNITY KNOCKS

The world might not take its threats seriously, but Iran has made no secret of its ambitions. Iran's leaders want to re-create the Persian Empire of old, but with an Islamic twist. They desire an arc of Shiite control stretching from Iran to the Mediterranean. They hope to become the dominant Muslim power in the Middle East, exerting influence and perhaps even control over their traditional Sunni rivals. But to reach that goal they need to find a way to eliminate Israel.

And that is where Iran's desires may intersect Bible prophecy.

The last time Persia was featured in Bible prophecy was when Daniel the prophet announced the rise of a nation, pictured as a ram, charging in conquest "toward the west and the north and the south" (Dan. 8:4). God made sure Daniel knew the identity of the kingdom that within eight years would destroy the nation of Babylon. "The two-horned ram that you saw represents the kings of Media and Persia" (v. 20). But God then announced the kingdom that would destroy the Medo-Persian Empire two centuries later. A goat from the west would race across the world to attack and destroy the ram. And God explained to Daniel that the goat represented "the king of Greece" (v. 21). And just as God announced, Alexander the Great raced across the globe and conquered the Medo-Persian Empire in three epic battles.

While Daniel predicted a Persian Empire that is now long gone, the prophet Ezekiel had previously announced a walk-on role for a new Persian Empire when he declared:

> The word of the LORD came to me: "Son of man, set your
> face against Gog, of the land of Magog, the chief prince of

Meshek and Tubal; prophesy against him and say: 'This is what the Sovereign LORD says: I am against you, Gog, chief prince of Meshek and Tubal. I will turn you around, put hooks in your jaws and bring you out with your whole army—your horses, your horsemen fully armed, and a great horde with large and small shields, all of them brandishing their swords. Persia, Cush and Put will be with them, all with shields and helmets.'" (Ezek. 38:1–5)

In today's parlance Iran's role in this future drama is just a "bit part," but the battle that unfolds, according to Ezekiel, is one of epic proportions. And the prophet predicted this still-future invasion against Israel by a man he called "Gog" who assembles a multinational coalition that includes the land of Persia (v. 5). And ancient Persia is modern-day Iran.

The leader who assembles his coalition for a surprise attack against Israel has a diverse cast of characters in his army. In Ezekiel 38:5 the prophet records three distinct members of this alliance: "Persia, Cush and Put will be with them, all with shields and helmets." These three nations represent the western, southern, and eastern extremities, respectively, of a coalition whose main body, as we learned earlier, is to the north. And since the three are said to be advancing "with them," it appears they will send forces to join the main body of invaders from the north.

What could possibly induce Iran to align with a leader from Russia? Actually, Iran and Russia have been trading partners for several decades, and much of Iran's military hardware comes from Russia. The two countries are also strategic allies in their fight to keep Bashar al-Assad in power in Syria. It's more difficult to understand Iran's connection to the other countries in this coalition, especially those dominated by Sunnis. But perhaps their focus on a common enemy helps them overcome their deep religious differences. As an old Sanskrit proverb says, "The enemy of my enemy is my friend."

Iran's hatred for Israel is a matter of religious conviction. They have invested uncounted billions in terror organizations and ever-more-deadly weapons of destruction, much of it intended to be used against Israel. Iran also knows its limitations and Israel's strengths, and that has kept it from pushing Israel too far. But if Iran were ever given an opportunity to be part of a massive coalition mobilizing against Israel, their leaders would jump at the chance.

Ezekiel predicted that's exactly what they will do—when the time is right.

FIVE

PICKING UP THE PIECES

The Destabilization of Europe

And just as you saw the iron mixed with baked clay,
so the people will be a mixture and will not remain
united, any more than iron mixes with clay.
—DANIEL 2:43

The first two decades of the twenty-first century haven't been kind to the European Union. The European Union was formally established in 1993 as a confederation of nations sharing a common parliament, common currency, free trade, and open borders. The initial union of six states ballooned to twenty-eight, and the euro became a major world currency. But the integration wasn't as seamless as the initial architects had hoped.

The worldwide economic crisis in late 2007 highlighted

the structural flaws in the European Union. On paper Europe was a union of twenty-eight equal states, but in reality the European Union was divided economically into have and have-not states. After several years of financial difficulty, Germany and the northern EU countries returned to a period of solid economic growth and prosperity. Unfortunately, many of the countries in the southern half of the European Union remain mired in economic recession and stagnation.

The economic cracks within the European Union generated a new vocabulary. The "Grexit," or Greek exit from the European Union, became a specter haunting the halls of power in the European Union. The fear was that such an event could trigger a domino effect across the southern half of the Eurozone, impacting other struggling EU countries, such as Italy, Spain, and Portugal.

And then, just as the threat of Grexit diminished, Brexit arose—the British withdrawal from the European Union. The chief motivation behind Brexit was the fear that continuing unlimited immigration would overwhelm Britain's already-stretched social services. Stratfor, a geopolitical intelligence and consulting firm, analyzed Britain's perspective on the European Union, which ultimately led to their vote to withdraw. "From London's point of view, the European Union should be a structure based on free trade and political agreements, not necessarily on the free movement of people or on a commitment to surrender sovereignty to unelected officials in Brussels."[1] When Britain voted to leave the European Union on June 23, 2016, the reverberations were felt internationally.

The European Union is struggling to keep its member states politically united and economically sound. But even as some states threaten to leave, others are pounding at the door, demanding admittance. At the front of the line is Turkey, a country with 77 million Muslim citizens.

Turkey has sought membership in the European Union for almost three decades, but their application has been held up by concerns over their record on human rights. "Negotiations in earnest began in 2005, when it was made clear that Turkey would not be admitted until it made serious progress in democratization and improved its dismal record on human rights."[2] Europe's concerns are reflected in the lack of progress made thus far. Turkey and the European Union have begun discussions on only fifteen of the thirty-five policy areas required to join.[3]

Turkey's admission to the European Union poses difficult questions that many in Europe have been unwilling to address. Can an Islamic-majority country mesh with the cultural traditions of the West? Would eliminating border controls bring about greater Western influence on Turkey or a greater Islamic influence on the West? The questions are as uncomfortable as the answers are elusive.

THE PROBLEM OF EUROPE

The European Union was, in many ways, intended as the continent's counterpart to the United States of America—a federal structure designed to bind the individual states together. The United States shares a common currency. Citizens can travel freely between states. Citizens of one state can work in another and relocate there without receiving governmental permission. Americans take such privileges for granted, but until the formation of the European Union, the experience of Europeans was far different. Visiting a neighboring state meant passing through border control and customs and converting funds into another currency. A European Union patterned in part on the United States made sense, at least on paper.

So why hasn't the European Union worked as well in practice? Three basic problems have kept the European Union from becoming a unified Europe.

The most basic problem remains the deeply engrained cultural and linguistic barriers separating the different countries. The United States was forged from thirteen relatively recent colonies that shared common linguistic, historical, and cultural ties to England. In contrast, the different states in Europe have existed as autonomous nations for centuries with their own unique languages, histories, and cultures. Modern trade, travel, and communication—especially radio, television, and the Internet—have lowered those barriers. But each country's cultural DNA remains deeply imprinted on its citizens.

A second problem keeping Europe from achieving unity is a growing economic disparity. As mentioned earlier, Europe is divided into two large groups, with northern European countries experiencing greater growth and lower unemployment while those countries in the south struggle with high unemployment and stagnating economies. Garret Martin, a specialist in European affairs, captured the complexity of the problem:

> Divisions are an unfortunate reality of Europe's DNA. For much of its history, the continent's aspirations for peace and unity have fallen prey to disputes and wars over religion, politics, or ideology to name a few. The European Union's current woes are the latest example, with the ongoing Eurozone crisis undermining the ideal of integration as ancient centrifugal forces emerge anew. On the surface, the current divide reflects contrasting economic fortunes, with the Southern European states (particularly Italy, Spain, Greece and Portugal) disproportionately impacted by the Eurozone debt crisis, and forced to rely on substantial economic relief from the wealthier Northern European states.[4]

In reality, the reasons for such economic disparity are incredibly complex. But the result is that the EU countries north of the Alps perceive the causes and cures for Europe's economic woes far differently than the countries south of the Alps. Just as in marital relationships, differing perceptions of—and approaches to—finances between nations can create conflicts. As has been observed, "If marriage is all about love, then divorce is all about money."[5]

The third problem keeping Europe fractured is the policy on unlimited immigration. The Schengen Area, as planned, made perfect economic sense. Individuals from any country in the European Union would be free to live and work in any other EU country without the need of a visa or work permit. Unfortunately, the agreement has been stretched to the breaking point by the intensifying migrant crisis.

For centuries, Europe has experienced an influx of migrants from Africa, the Middle East, and the Far East. Much of this migration was the result of Europe's colonial expansion. Dr. Pieter Emmer and Dr. Leo Lucassen specialize in studying migration history at Leiden University, and they have traced the causes for the influx of migrants to Europe, saying:

> Colonialism not only stimulated more than 60 million Europeans to migrate overseas, it also brought millions of Asians, Africans and Amerindians to Europe. In the beginning, many of these immigrants came to Europe as slaves, but in the 20th century immigrants from Africa and Asia served as soldiers and contract labourers in the European armies during the two World Wars.[6]

More recently, migrants have fled to Europe from wartorn regions in Africa and the Middle East. The civil war in Syria forced more than six million Syrians to flee their homes. Almost five million of those have moved to other countries, with almost 60 percent crossing the border into Turkey. Some made their way into western Turkey, where, after a short but dangerous boat ride, they washed up on one of the many Greek islands. Others traveled overland past Istanbul toward Greece or Bulgaria. Once inside these EU countries, they either tried to blend in or to claim political asylum. In 2015 alone nearly three hundred thousand Syrian refugees sought asylum in the European Union.

Europe has struggled to care for the overwhelming numbers of refugees, especially with the ongoing financial crisis already straining its resources. And compounding the financial and social pressures was the fear that ISIS was smuggling operatives into Europe among the refugees. One ISIS operative claimed that as many as four thousand jihadists had been embedded among those fleeing Syria.[7] And the fact that the terrorist attacks in Paris, Brussels, and Istanbul included ISIS fighters drove home the plausibility of such claims.

No doubt about it, the European Union seems to have fallen on hard times. Raf Casert, Associated Press news editor in Benelux, summarized the words of EU president Donald Tusk:

> After decades of often unbridled expansion and increasing prosperity, the once-robust European Union is . . . looking at its biggest challenge—crumbling from within.[8]

But is the European Union's obituary about to be written, or might the Bible point Europe in a different, more sinister, direction?

DANIEL'S VISION OF THE FUTURE

The prophet Daniel was taken from Jerusalem into exile in Babylon. He experienced firsthand the decline and fall of the kingdom of Judah and the rise of the first of a series of Gentile empires that would rule over the land God had promised to Israel. In a dramatic series of prophecies, Daniel pictured in great detail the events that would unfold during the "times of the Gentiles" that would last until the Messiah finally arrived to inaugurate God's promised kingdom.

In chapters 2–7 Daniel switched from Hebrew to Aramaic, the international language of that day, to emphasize this time when the Jewish people will be subject to Gentile domination. He arranged his material in a chiastic literary structure that was relatively common in ancient Jewish writings, though not well understood by readers today. The structure is characterized by arranging ideas in a parallel fashion. In the six Aramaic chapters of Daniel 2–7, the first and last chapters are parallel, chapters 3 and 6 are parallel, and chapters 4 and 5 are parallel. The structure looks something like this:

A. Prophecy about four Gentile nations and God's
   kingdom (chapter 2)
   B. Persecution/deliverance of God's followers (chapter 3)
      C. God's revelation to Babylon's first king (chapter 4)
      C.' God's revelation to Babylon's last king (chapter 5)
   B.' Persecution/deliverance of God's followers (chapter 6)
A.' Prophecy about four Gentile nations and God's
   kingdom (chapter 7)

Chapters 2 and 7 focus on a series of four Gentile kingdoms that will arise between the time of Daniel and the time the Messiah arrives to set up His kingdom. The four kingdoms are pictured as four parts of a giant statue in chapter 2 and as four beasts in chapter 7. Daniel identified the statue's head of gold as Nebuchadnezzar when he proclaimed:

> Your Majesty, you are the king of kings. The God of heaven has given you dominion and power and might and glory; in your hands he has placed all mankind and the beasts of the field and the birds in the sky. Wherever they live, he has made you ruler over them all. You are that head of gold. (Dan. 2:37–38)

He then said the next part of the statue pictures "another kingdom," and the third points to "a third kingdom" that "will rule over the whole earth" (v. 39). The fourth part of the statue, made of iron, represents a fourth empire that will be in control when God sends a stone to smash the statue. The stone represents a "kingdom that will never be destroyed" (v. 44). The four beasts in chapter 7 correspond to the four empires in chapter 2. But if Nebuchadnezzar and the Babylonian Empire are the first in this series of empires, who are the remaining three?

Historically, we know that the Babylonian Empire was destroyed by Cyrus, the head of the Medo-Persian Empire. Medo-Persia was the next empire to extend its control over Jerusalem and the Jewish people. It was eventually conquered by Alexander the Great, ruler of the Greek Empire. Daniel actually confirmed this sequence of empire in a subsequent vision:

I am going to tell you what will happen later in the time of wrath, because the vision concerns the appointed time of the end. The two-horned ram that you saw represents the kings of Media and Persia. The shaggy goat is the king of Greece, and the large horn between its eyes is the first king. (Dan. 8:19–21)

Babylon, Medo-Persia, Greece. Three of the four Gentile empires are identified by name in the book of Daniel. But what is the final empire that is to rise before God brings His promised kingdom? History—and Daniel—supply the answer.

Historically, the empire that conquered the territory once controlled by Greece was Rome. Rome was also the power in control of the promised land when Jesus arrived as Israel's promised Messiah. History points to the Roman Empire as the fourth empire in Daniel's vision.

Daniel provides confirmation of this in chapter 9. He received a detailed historical time line of history from the issuing of a command to rebuild Jerusalem after the Babylonian captivity, through the first coming of the Messiah, and on into a still-future, seven-year period of trouble that will culminate in the arrival of God's promised kingdom. Following the arrival of the promised Messiah, God announced that this "Anointed One" would be "put to death," which is exactly what happened to Jesus.

God then said, "The people of the ruler who will come will destroy the city and the sanctuary" (v. 26). The actions of this still-future ruler are then described in verse 27. But note carefully that this future individual is identified by what happened to Jerusalem following the death of the Messiah. It was this ruler's "people" who destroyed Jerusalem and the temple after the Messiah was cut off. And who destroyed Jerusalem following the death of Jesus?

The Romans.

The Roman Empire held firm control during the first coming of the Messiah, and the Roman Empire will again be present and in control at the time of Christ's second coming. Five hundred years after Daniel shared God's prediction, Jesus announced that the details of Daniel 9:27 were still future (Matt. 24:15–16). Later, the apostle John described the future Antichrist as the fourth beast/empire from Daniel 7. (Compare Revelation 13:1–10 with Daniel 7:7–8, 23–25.)[9]

A revived Roman Empire will rule the earth before Christ's return.

But that leads to perhaps the most remarkable prediction of all about this fourth kingdom. In Daniel 2 the prophet actually described two phases of this kingdom. In the first phase, the legs of the empire are as "strong as iron—for iron breaks and smashes everything" (v. 40). But when Daniel pictured the final part of the statue, the "feet and toes," a major transformation took place.

The feet and toes of the statue are not solid iron. Instead they are "partly of baked clay and partly of iron" (v. 41). Trying to somehow mold together clay and iron would be an exercise in futility. Iron doesn't combine with clay. The vision is of an entity that is inherently unstable and fragile. But in what way? God provided the answer with His interpretation:

> "This will be a divided kingdom; yet it will have some of the strength of iron in it, even as you saw iron mixed with clay. As the toes were partly iron and partly clay, so this kingdom will be partly strong and partly brittle. And just as you saw the iron mixed with baked clay, so the people will be a mixture and will not remain united, any more than iron mixes with clay." (vv. 41–43)

The characteristics of this final empire are remarkable. It will have the strength of iron, yet somehow be brittle. In its initial form this fourth kingdom has legs that are made of iron, picturing the kingdom's military might and ability to "crush and break all the others" (v. 40). But in its final form, though still possessing the military strength of iron, the kingdom will have a brittleness about it, an inherent weakness that will create problems. And that weakness is pictured as a lack of internal unity among the people who comprise the kingdom. Dr. Leon Wood summarized the interpretation God provided to Daniel:

> As baked clay and iron will not mix, so also these diverse elements will not mix. This means that the empire of the Antichrist will have its internal problems, making for weakness.[10]

Iron combined with clay. Strong but weak. Militarily capable but lacking coherence. Such is the description of the kingdom over which the Antichrist will rule. But how can anyone rule such a diverse group of people? Isn't it the political equivalent of herding cats? Could this picture a fractured European Union, certainly formidable militarily—even in its weakened state—but eerily vulnerable culturally and financially?

From a human perspective it is impossible to bring unity and order to such a diverse group. Napoleon tried, and failed. Hitler tried, and failed. The European Union continues to try. But again the Bible explains how one man will be able to bring order out of chaos—to bring cohesion to something as diverse as iron mixed with clay. It will take supernatural intervention from the Prince of Darkness himself!

The Antichrist will be able to accomplish the impossible because he will be possessed and empowered by a force more powerful than anything devised by humanity. "The dragon [Satan] gave the beast his power and his throne and great authority" (Rev. 13:2). Satan's ultimate counterfeit will be to present a counterfeit Christ who will rule over a counterfeit kingdom.

> People worshiped the dragon because he had given author-
> ity to the beast, and they also worshiped the beast and
> asked, "Who is like the beast? Who can wage war against
> it?" (v. 4)

Europe might be fractured, but Satan thrives best in disunity, disharmony, and discord. An empire will once again arise from the area once ruled by Rome. And it will bring the world to its knees.

SIX

ISRAEL

The Eye of the Hurricane

On that day, when all the nations of the earth
are gathered against her, I will make Jerusalem
an immovable rock for all the nations. All who
try to move it will injure themselves.

—ZECHARIAH 12:3

God's promised program for Israel forms one of the central themes of the Bible. Entire volumes, such as Arnold Fruchtenbaum's thousand-page masterpiece *Israelology*, focus in great detail on the subject.[1] Understanding the clash of kingdoms would be incomplete without exploring Israel's central role in this future drama.

From a human perspective Israel ought to occupy nothing more than a minor supporting part in any worldwide drama. In terms of geographical size, Israel ranks 148th among the nations of the world, nestled between Belize and El Salvador. Her standing improves slightly when ranked by population. At just over eight million, Israel breaks the top 100, coming in 98th between Switzerland and Honduras. And when comparing gross domestic product (GDP), Israel is ranked between 34th and 37th, depending on which organization is doing the measuring. Still, that puts Israel in with countries such as Malaysia, Singapore, and Hong Kong with barely one-quarter the GDP of a country like Mexico.

God, however, uses a different standard of measurement. And in His eyes Israel ranks at the top of the list in terms of national significance.

> "For you are a people holy to the LORD your God. The LORD your God has chosen you out of all the peoples on the face of the earth to be his people, his treasured possession. The LORD did not set his affection on you and choose you because you were more numerous than other peoples, for you were the fewest of all peoples. But it was because the LORD loved you and kept the oath he swore to your ancestors." (Deut. 7:6–8)

> "Out of all the peoples on the face of the earth, the LORD has chosen you to be his treasured possession." (Deut. 14:2)

> "If you fully obey the LORD your God and carefully follow all his commands I give you today, the LORD your God will set you high above all the nations on earth." (Deut. 28:1)

God gave Israel the title to a specific plot of land. He provided a general description of its boundaries to Abraham:

> "To your descendants I give this land, from the Wadi of Egypt to the great river, the Euphrates." (Gen. 15:18)

Later, as Israel prepared to enter that promised land, God gave more detailed land boundaries (Num. 34:1–12).

Some believe God's promises to Israel were fulfilled in the past and therefore don't require a future fulfillment. But after Israel was taken out of the land into captivity, God gave updated land boundaries and said they will be fulfilled when He brings Israel back into the land in the future (Ezek. 47:13–20). Israel is the only nation in the world to whom God conveyed clear title to a specific piece of real estate!

God also announced that the reign of Israel's promised Messiah would extend over the nations of the world and bring universal peace.

> *He will judge between the nations*
> *and will settle disputes for many peoples.*
> *They will beat their swords into plowshares*
> *and their spears into pruning hooks.*
> *Nation will not take up sword against nation,*
> *nor will they train for war anymore.* (Isa. 2:4)

The New Testament describes the time when this will be fulfilled. Jesus will return to earth and will " 'rule them with an iron scepter'. . . . On his robe and on his thigh he has this name written: KING OF KINGS AND LORD OF LORDS" (Rev. 19:15–16).

God's promises are amazing, but they also seem disconnected from what's actually taking place today. Israel controls *some* of the land promised to her by God, but not all. And the United Nations repeatedly condemns Israel for not relinquishing control over a significant portion of the land she does control. Israel might be stronger than the surrounding nations of the Middle East, but the region still has an abundance of swords and a dearth of plowshares. So what must happen before the Messiah returns? Or, more specifically, what must happen *in Israel* before the Messiah returns?

THINGS TO COME

The Bible presents four key signposts that provide directions for Israel's future. And each signpost helps explain the central role Israel will play in resolving the conflict among the kingdoms.

Signpost #1: Israel and Jerusalem will become more problematic for the world.

If the United Nations General Assembly were used as the yardstick, Israel would appear to be the most dangerous and diabolical nation on the face of the earth. During the General Assembly's 70th session in 2015, a total of twenty-three resolutions were passed condemning various countries of the world. Iran, Syria, and North Korea were each singled out once for criticism over violations of human rights. The remaining twenty resolutions condemned Israel.[2]

As Eric Mandel opined in the *Jerusalem Post*:

> Israel is the only nation in the world that has a standing agenda item against it at every session of the UNHRC [United Nations Human Rights Council]. Not North Korea, not China, not Pakistan, not Syria, not Sudan, not Iran.[3]

The United Nations seems to have a bias against Israel. Perhaps that's to be expected with the large number of Muslim countries in the United Nations. But America's changing attitude toward Israel is more worrisome. Michael Oren, former Israeli ambassador to the United States, described that change as a shift in perception on the part of the United States, a change in what America perceives to be the key underlying problem in the Middle East.

> The notion of linkage is practically doctrinal in the Obama administration. What does linkage mean? That if you solve the Arab-Israeli conflict, you will solve a whole series of other conflicts in the Middle East. . . .
>
> So if you believe that the Arab-Israeli conflict is the core conflict, and the core of that conflict is what the administration calls the Israeli occupation and the settlements, then that leads you, obviously, to the conclusion that you

have to force Israel to give up the settlements, to talk about a two-state solution, to stop building parts of Jerusalem.[4]

Whether the message originates in the United Nations, the United States, France, England, or some other country or international body, the consensus today is that an agreement between Israel and the Palestinians is essential for resolving all the problems of the Middle East. It doesn't matter that the conflicts in Syria, Iraq, Egypt, Libya, Yemen, or Turkey have *nothing* to do with Israel and the Palestinians. The problem is *always* said to be the conflict between Israel and the Palestinians . . . and the party to blame is *always* Israel.

Outside attempts to resolve the Israeli-Palestinian conflict only seem to make matters worse. The French held an international conference to promote an Israeli-Palestinian peace process. Curiously, they chose not to invite Israel or the Palestinians. And predictably, the conference concluded that violence and Israeli settlement growth were endangering a permanent solution. Following the conference Palestinian president Mahmoud Abbas called for full Israeli withdrawal to the 1967 cease-fire lines—temporary armistice lines from the 1948 War of Independence that were to be replaced by negotiated permanent borders. At that time, however, no Arab state was willing to negotiate final borders with Israel.

Five hundred years before the first coming of Jesus, the prophet Zechariah described a sequence of events that will lead to His second coming. And the first event on Zechariah's list is a growing animosity toward Israel on the part of other nations. At the heart of the anger is a desire on the part of these nations to control the land of Judah and the city of Jerusalem. And the harder they try, the more they will fail.

In Zechariah 12:2–3, God said:

"I am going to make Jerusalem a cup that sends all the surrounding peoples reeling. Judah will be besieged as well as Jerusalem. On that day, when all the nations of the earth are gathered against her, I will make Jerusalem an immovable rock for all the nations. All who try to move it will injure themselves."

From the world's perspective Israel appears intransigent and obstinate. But all their attempts to dislodge the Jewish people from their promised land only seem to create greater problems for the aggressors. Someday that will change. A world leader will arise and succeed where all others have failed.

Signpost #2: Israel will agree to a seven-year peace treaty.

Countless presidents and prime ministers have tried to solve the Israeli-Palestinian conflict. And thus far all have failed. Oslo. Camp David. The Quartet. The Arab Peace Initiative. The Paris Peace Conference. The one constant is the apparent agreement by all outside parties that Israel and the Palestinians can't resolve the issues on their own. Progress has only taken place when the two sides have been prodded by those from the outside. And, of course, most of the prodding seems to be directed at Israel.

Previous attempts to resolve the issues have involved outside nations using incentives to induce Israelis and Palestinians
to sit down together and negotiate. This approach has failed.
The French tried a new approach. Their conference invited
everyone *but* the Israelis and Palestinians. Their goal was to
build an international consensus that would push the two sides
toward an agreement. But as Matthew Duss, president of the
Foundation for Middle East Peace, noted, this new approach
also fell short:

> It's fine to reaffirm the international consensus behind
> the two-state solution and warn against steps that under-
> mine it, but *without the serious prospect of consequences for
> those violations*, it's difficult to see how any improvement
> in the negotiating environment—an ostensible goal of this
> effort—will be achieved.[5]

So what will it take to achieve peace? Perhaps a treaty
forged by an outside power that is strong enough to enforce
the treaty's conditions and compromises. A treaty affirmed
by many nations, not just Israel and the Palestinians. A treaty
with a specific road map and timetable to be followed by all
participants. A treaty that will appear to resolve—once and for
all—this thorniest of conflicts in the Middle East. A treaty that
will promise lasting peace between Israel and all her immediate neighbors. A treaty predicted in the Bible.

In Daniel 9 God sent the angel Gabriel to give Daniel a
detailed prophetic timeline for Israel. The 490-year timeline

began with a command to restore and build Jerusalem. Gabriel told Daniel the first 483 years would extend until the arrival of "the Anointed One, the ruler" (v. 25). The Hebrew word for "Anointed One" is *mashiach*, Messiah. In a detailed study of the prophecy, the late Dr. Harold Hoehner determined that the command to restore and rebuild Jerusalem was issued on March 5, 444 BC, and extended to March 30, AD 33, the very day Jesus rode into Jerusalem as the Messiah.[6]

God then inserted a gap into Daniel's prophetic timeline. After the arrival of the Messiah, but before the start of the final seven-year period, God told Daniel three events would happen:

> "The Anointed One will be put to death and will have nothing. The people of the ruler who will come will destroy the city and the sanctuary. The end will come like a flood: War will continue until the end, and desolations have been decreed." (v. 26)

The Messiah would be killed. Less than a week after His triumphal entry, Jesus was put to death on the cross. After this event Jerusalem and the temple would again be destroyed. This happened in AD 70 when the Roman army breached the walls of Jerusalem. And finally, the subsequent interim period would be marked by "war" and "desolation." The prophecy is focusing on the Jewish people, and these words are a sad reflection of the horrors faced by the Jewish people during the past two thousand years.

One final seven-year period remains before the prophecy is completely fulfilled. And God told Daniel the specific event that will start the prophetic clock ticking one last time: "He will confirm a covenant with many for one 'seven'" (v. 27). The "he" refers back to the "ruler who will come" in the previous verse. He is identified in part by his ethnic association. His "people" were the ones who destroyed Jerusalem following the cutting off of the Messiah. The Romans destroyed Jerusalem, so this is referring to a future leader who will arise from the revived Roman Empire, discussed in the previous chapter.

This future world leader will be clearly identified through one signature event. He will confirm, or make firm, an agreement. He will succeed in bringing to fruition a treaty or alliance. Though Daniel was not told the specific nature of the treaty, he was told that it will be made with "many." It's not simply an agreement between two individuals. It will encompass numerous parties.

One additional New Testament passage hints at the nature of this agreement. In 1 Thessalonians 5, Paul described the sudden arrival of the day of the Lord, a time of trouble that will come on the whole world. Paul told the church in Thessalonica that this time of trouble will come unexpectedly on a world that is actually anticipating just the opposite:

While people are saying, "Peace and safety," destruction will come on them suddenly. (v. 3)

As the end times begin, people will be expecting a time of peace and safety. Could this sense of optimism result from the signing of a long-sought peace treaty between Israel and her neighbors? A firm agreement, backed up by the might of a rising world power? An agreement between many? An agreement that will be implemented over a seven-year period? An agreement—as we will see—that will be viciously violated and broken a mere three and a half years after it is signed?

Signpost #3: Israel will experience religious revival.

Israel's third signpost will be a sudden, dramatic religious revival. Though it may come as a surprise to some, many of the "Chosen People" now living in the "Holy Land" are not very religious. In a poll conducted several years ago, Israelis were asked to define themselves religiously. According to Israel's Central Bureau of Statistics, 8 percent of Israeli adults defined themselves as ultra-Orthodox, 13 percent as religious, 13 percent as traditional-religious, 25 percent as traditional but "not very religious," and 42 percent as secular.[7] Two-thirds of Israelis see themselves as either "not very religious" or totally secular.

But the Bible says that will change in at least four specific ways.

First, Israel will rebuild its temple. The apostle John wrote the book of Revelation about twenty years after the armies of Rome had destroyed Jerusalem and the temple. Yet in Revelation 11:1 he was told to "measure the temple of God and the altar, with its worshipers." In 2 Thessalonians 2:4 the apostle Paul identified the coming "man of lawlessness" (v. 3) as an individual who "will oppose and will exalt himself over everything that is called God or is worshiped, so that he *sets himself up in God's temple*, proclaiming himself to be God" (italics added). For this to happen, a new temple has to be built.

Second, Israel will experience a revival of prophets and prophecy. After measuring the new temple, the apostle John then describes the prophetic activity of two "witnesses" who will walk the streets of Jerusalem for three and a half years (Rev. 11:3–6). The miracles they perform parallel the past ministries of Moses and Elijah. God will raise up new prophets like those of old.

Third, individuals will respond to God and become dramatic followers of Jesus. Jesus had twelve disciples whom He sent out to the lost sheep of the house of Israel. But in the final days God will raise up a spiritual army to go out as His ambassadors into the entire world. John described it this way:

> "Do not harm the land or the sea or the trees until we put a seal on the foreheads of the servants of our God." Then I heard the number of those who were sealed: 144,000 from all the tribes of Israel. (Rev. 7:3–4)

How successful are these evangelists? Apparently their impact will be felt around the world.

After this I looked, and there before me was a great multitude that no one could count, from every nation, tribe, people and language, standing before the throne and before the Lamb. (v. 9)

Finally, Israel itself will experience a national revival unlike anything it has experienced before. No doubt part of the revival will come in response to the ministry of the two prophetic witnesses in Jerusalem and the 144,000 ambassadors sent throughout the world.

Another part of the revival will come in response to God's miraculous deliverance from a surprise attack. After describing the battle and its aftermath, Ezekiel highlighted the impact it will have on Israel: "From that day forward the people of Israel will know that I am the LORD their God" (Ezek. 39:22). That battle marks a turning point in God's relationship with His people. Ezekiel ended his description of the battle with this promise from God:

"I will no longer hide my face from them, for I will pour out my Spirit on the people of Israel," declares the Sovereign LORD. (v. 29)

The prophet Zechariah described this time of revival and spiritual restoration in words that are strikingly prophetic:

"And I will pour out on the house of David and the inhabitants of Jerusalem a spirit of grace and supplication. They will look on me, the one they have pierced, and they will mourn for him as one mourns for an only child, and grieve bitterly for him as one grieves for a firstborn son. . . . On that day a fountain will be opened to the house of David and the inhabitants of Jerusalem, to cleanse them from sin and impurity." (Zech. 12:10; 13:1)

The apostle Paul wrote about the same time of national revival:

I do not want you to be ignorant of this mystery, brothers and sisters, so that you may not be conceited: Israel has experienced a hardening in part until the full number of the Gentiles has come in, *and in this way all Israel will be saved.* As it is written:

> *"The deliverer will come from Zion;*
>   *he will turn godlessness away from Jacob."*
> (Rom. 11:25–26, italics added)

Paul was not saying that every single Jewish person will come to believe in Jesus. But the revival will be so dramatic it will be as if the entire nation turns to Him.

Great things spiritually are in store for Israel in the future. But those spiritual blessings will come during a time of great national calamity. And that leads to the final signpost offering direction regarding Israel's future and its conflict between the nations.

Signpost #4: Israel will be attacked and rescued.

Israel will be pressured into signing an agreement that will appear to offer peace. That peace will be threatened early on by a surprise attack that will be halted by the God of heaven—not the human leader who promised peace and safety. The list of weapons in God's heavenly arsenal are ancient but potent. God will first use an earthquake to stop the invaders in their tracks, as we learn in Ezekiel 38:

> "This is what will happen in that day: When Gog attacks the land of Israel, my hot anger will be aroused, declares the Sovereign LORD. In my zeal and fiery wrath I declare that at that time there shall be a great earthquake in the land of Israel." (vv. 18–19)

The earthquake will devastate the roads and bridges being used by the invading forces. How severe will it be? "The mountains will be overturned, the cliffs will crumble and every wall will fall to the ground" (v. 20). In the resulting confusion God unleashes His second weapon—a devastating panic that causes this multinational invasion force to start fighting among themselves. "Every man's sword will be against his brother" (v. 21).

But God has not yet exhausted His heavenly armory. Imagine this terrifying scene unfolding:

> "I will execute judgment on him with plague and bloodshed; I will pour down torrents of rain, hailstones and

burning sulfur on him and on his troops and on the many nations with him." (v. 22)

The wounded can't be evacuated or treated because of the devastated infrastructure. And then flooding begins and large hailstones rain down on the ragged remains of this once-mighty army. And as final punctuation, God sends "burning sulfur," perhaps describing a volcanic eruption or destruction similar to the one that destroyed Sodom and Gomorrah. The northern approach to Israel, across the Golan Heights, is punctuated with volcanic peaks, testimony to similar activity in the past.

A few years after this attack, Israel's promised peace will be shattered once again. And this time it will be at the hand of the very one who originally came offering peace.

The prophet Daniel was one of the first to describe the future troubles Israel will face. Having announced the confirmation of a covenant designed to run for seven years, Daniel explained how it will be violated:

> In the middle of the "seven" he will put an end to sacrifice and offering. And at the temple he will set up an abomination that causes desolation, until the end that is decreed is poured out on him. (Dan. 9:27)

The treaty is broken, the temple sacrifices are ended, and something abominable will be set up until God finally puts a stop to this monster's madness.

Daniel's prophecy describes a time of stress and struggle,

though it is somewhat vague. Jesus Himself, however, explained in greater detail the meaning of Daniel's words, and their impact on the people of the land:

> "So when you see standing in the holy place 'the abomination that causes desolation,' spoken of through the prophet Daniel—let the reader understand—then let those who are in Judea flee to the mountains. Let no one on the housetop go down to take anything out of the house. Let no one in the field go back to get their cloak. How dreadful it will be in those days for pregnant women and nursing mothers! Pray that your flight will not take place in winter or on the Sabbath. For then there will be great distress, unequaled from the beginning of the world until now—and never to be equaled again." (Matt. 24:15–21)

When the "abomination that causes desolation" is standing in the Holy Place—the temple—that is the sign for the people of Israel to flee as quickly as possible. Jesus said that event will signal the start of a time of persecution and distress that has never been matched in world history. And when you think back to some of the past horrors of history, Jesus' words can send a shiver down your spine.

Two passages help explain in more detail the "abomination that causes desolation." The first, mentioned earlier, is 2 Thessalonians 2:4, in which Paul described the activity of the coming man of lawlessness. Paul said he "sets himself up in God's temple, proclaiming himself to be God."

The second passage is Revelation 13. John described the beast who will "utter proud words and blasphemies and . . . exercise its authority for forty-two months" (v. 5). He is accompanied by a "second beast," whose role is to get the world to worship this leader. He "ordered them to set up an image in honor of the beast" (v. 14). Perhaps this statue, which appears to come to life, is the abomination of desolation. It is certainly an abomination. And the command to kill all who refuse to bow down and worship it will bring great desolation on all who refuse.

Individual persecution will eventually become an all-out attack on God's people. The armies of the Antichrist will begin a campaign to crush all remaining opposition. The task force will assemble in the Jezreel Valley by the hill of Megiddo. "Then they gathered the kings together to the place that in Hebrew is called Armageddon" (Rev. 16:16). Daniel 11:41–45 describes the campaign that follows. The initial incursion into the "Beautiful Land" (Israel) is followed by a North African campaign against Egypt, Libya, and Cush (the region of southern Egypt and Sudan). Reports from the east and north cause alarm, and this evil coalition quickly heads in that direction.

Having vanquished all these other foes, the Antichrist's army eventually pivots and advances on its final objective. "He will pitch his royal tents between the seas at the beautiful holy mountain" (Dan. 11:45). The two "seas" are the Mediterranean Sea and the Dead Sea, and the "beautiful holy mountain" in between is Jerusalem—Mount Zion. The final objective is to capture Jerusalem and destroy the Jewish remnant holding out there.

Perhaps the Antichrist sees this as a replay of the Roman attack in AD 70. Perhaps he is overconfident or blinded by Satan's venomous rage. But what he anticipates to be his final march to victory, God has already declared to be his summons to destruction:

> I will gather all the nations to Jerusalem to fight against it. . . . Then the LORD will go out and fight against those nations, as he fights on a day of battle. On that day his feet will stand on the Mount of Olives, east of Jerusalem. (Zech. 14:2–4)

Israel's future will take her into the eye of the hurricane as clashing kingdoms collide across the earth. But the eye of the hurricane can prove to be a much safer place than those being lashed by the destructive winds swirling about on all sides.

SEVEN

A WOMAN IN A BASKET

The Rise of Babylon

"Where are they taking the basket?" I asked the angel
who was speaking to me. He replied, "To the country
of Babylonia to build a house for it. When the house
is ready, the basket will be set there in its place."
—ZECHARIAH 5:10–11

I magine that many of the events already described in this
book have taken place. ISIS has been degraded and finally
dislodged from Syria and Iraq. A peace agreement has been
forged between Israel and her neighbors. But the promised
peace was shattered when Russia, Iran, and Turkey, along
with their allies from North Africa, launched a surprise attack
against Israel—an attack that was repulsed. The invading
armies were destroyed in a rapid succession of supernatural

hammer blows. And, through a divinely orchestrated counter-strike, many of the lands of the invaders themselves were destroyed, as described to us in Ezekiel 39:6:

> "I will send fire on Magog and on those who live in safety in the coastlands, and they will know that I am the LORD."

What impact will this series of events have on Europe and the Middle East?

Europe emerges unscathed militarily, but it will suffer economically. Trade with Russia, Turkey, and Iran will be disrupted. The European Union is heavily dependent on Russian oil and natural gas. Dr. Robert Orttung, associate research professor at the Elliott School of International Affairs at George Washington University, described the extent of Europe's dependence on Russia:

> [Russia] is the European Union's third largest trade partner and its most important energy supplier. Russian oil and natural gas deliveries account for more than 25 percent of European consumption.[1]

The loss of Russian oil and natural gas would be a strategic blow to Europe, and that loss could be compounded by destruction in Iran and Turkey. Long term, Europe is hoping to tap into Iran's vast natural gas reserves by piping the gas through Turkey. Simone Tagliapietra, senior researcher at the Fondazione Eni Enrico Mattei, along with Dr. Georg

Zachmann, captured Europe's hopes for tapping into Iran's natural gas reserves:

> Iranian natural gas exports to the EU are no silver bullet. But, enabling an import route from Iran could have strategic value for Iran, Turkey and the EU.[2]

With the loss of Russian and Iranian energy supplies, Europe, and much of the Far East, would be scrambling to secure alternative sources of energy. And the commodities market might respond with a rapid, almost meteoric, rise in the price of oil. Oil-producing countries not impacted by the battle of Gog and Magog could once again have vast sums of money flowing into their national treasuries. And for the oil-rich countries of the Middle East, there might be one added bonus: they will no longer have to worry about Iran. The Shiite threat to the Sunnis would be eliminated. In fact, the two dominant non-Arab Muslim powers in the Middle East—Iran and Turkey—would both cease to be threats.

The immediate danger might be gone, but the Arab states in the Middle East, especially the oil-rich Gulf States, would not easily forget the turmoil and trouble that roiled the region. Calls for Arab unity have been sounded for decades, but none have succeeded because the benefits never outweighed the risks. The fear of future attacks, coupled with the dramatic increase in oil revenue, however, could finally convince them that an alliance is necessary for their survival, especially with so much of the world eyeing their precious oil and gas.

But where might the capital of this new alliance be located? Choosing an already-established capital might give too much power and prestige to one country in the alliance at the expense of others. Just as the newly minted United States of America made a political decision to found a new city, Washington, DC, as its capital, so an entirely new center of power might be more politically acceptable to these Arab states. But where should it be located?

What about Babylon?

EVERYTHING OLD IS NEW AGAIN

Babylon was both a city and an imperial capital. In the book of Daniel, Babylon was identified as the first in a series of four world powers that would control Israel and God's people. But Babylon didn't arise in a vacuum. A century before Nebuchadnezzar sat on his throne, the prophet Isaiah told King Hezekiah that Judah would be taken into captivity in Babylon:

> "The time will surely come when everything in your palace, and all that your predecessors have stored up until this day, will be carried off to Babylon. Nothing will be left," says the Lord. (Isa. 39:6)

God predicted the rise of Babylon long before it became a major power so Israel would know God was in control of history even when Babylon attacked and destroyed Jerusalem. God also announced that Babylon itself would be destroyed. When Isaiah proclaimed Babylon's destruction in Isaiah 13–14, Babylon was a second-rate, insignificant power, one of several nations controlled by the mighty Assyrian Empire. Yet Babylon was public enemy number one in Isaiah's list of nations God vowed to judge. Isaiah spent more time describing Babylon's fall than he did any other nation on the list. And the details of that judgment are significant.

Isaiah announced that Babylon would be judged in "the day of the LORD" (Isa. 13:6, 9). While there have been many days when God intervened in history, Isaiah predicted this day would be unique, involving supernatural signs in the heavens (v. 10) and divine judgment on the earth (v. 11). Isaiah also announced it would be a time when God would restore Israel to their land to "rule over their oppressors" (14:2). Babylon, meanwhile, would be "overthrown by God like Sodom and Gomorrah" (13:19), never to be inhabited again "through all generations" (v. 20).

From the day Isaiah made that prediction until today, his prophecy has remained unfulfilled.

THE GREATEST OF POWERS

A century after Isaiah made his prediction, Babylon was the greatest power in the Middle East. And that's when Jeremiah the prophet delivered another prophecy regarding Babylon

(Jer. 50–51). Jeremiah pictured a destruction in which the city would be torn apart and its people slaughtered. He called on any followers of God who happened to be there to "flee from Babylon! Run for your lives!" (Jer. 51:6).

Many believe Jeremiah's prophecy was fulfilled the night Babylon fell to Cyrus and the Medo-Persians. But this creates a problem. The prophet Daniel possessed a copy of the book of Jeremiah (Dan. 9:2), and he was living in Babylon the night the city fell (Dan. 5:30). Yet Daniel did *not* flee from the city. Was he disobedient? Or was he convinced this was not the fulfillment of Jeremiah's prophecy?

Jeremiah provided additional details that clearly were not fulfilled in Daniel's day. Twice during his prophecy against Babylon, Jeremiah used the phrase "In those days, at that time" (Jer. 50:4, 20). In both instances the prophet described events that did not happen in 539 BC. First, he said the Jewish people will return to the Lord both physically and spiritually. "They will ask the way to Zion and turn their faces toward it. They will come and bind themselves to the LORD in an everlasting covenant that will not be forgotten" (v. 5).

Second, Jeremiah predicted the Jewish people will experience national forgiveness of sin. "Search will be made for Israel's guilt, but there will be none, and for the sins of Judah, but none will be found, for I will forgive the remnant I spare" (v. 20).

Physical return, spiritual renewal, and forgiveness of sin. These promises are connected to the second coming of Jesus as Israel's promised Messiah (Zech. 12:10–13:1; Rom. 11:26–27).

But Jeremiah says that is *also* the time when Babylon will be destroyed!

Babylon did fall to Cyrus and the Medo-Persian Empire. Could this perhaps be a case where the Bible needs to be understood in a less-than-literal fashion? The city wasn't destroyed that night, although it did fall. Most inhabitants were spared, although the king was killed. Not all the Jewish people returned to the land, although some did. How do we know this *wasn't* the fulfillment of the prophecies of Isaiah and Jeremiah?

The answer can be found in an often-overlooked prophecy from the Old Testament book of Zechariah. Zechariah was one of the Jews who returned to the land following the fall of Babylon to Cyrus. He encouraged the people to rebuild the temple, and he delivered an amazing series of prophecies, some of which were fulfilled in remarkable detail by Jesus at His first coming. Zechariah also provided an astounding series of predictions that look toward Jesus' second coming. But hidden among the prophetic gems of this remarkable book is another message that is often overlooked.

In chapters 1–6, Zechariah shared a series of eight visions apparently revealed to him in a single night. The visions are arranged in a chiastic structure. All are important, but we want to explore the next to last of these eight revelations—the vision of a woman in a basket. In Zechariah 5:5–11, God's messenger showed the prophet an *ephah*, a measuring basket slightly smaller in size than a modern bushel basket. When Zechariah asked what the basket represented, the messenger's description at first seems rather confusing. He told the prophet, "This is the iniquity of the people throughout the land" (v. 6). A more literal translation is "This is their eye in all the land." In the Middle East the "evil eye" often refers to a jealous or malicious look that is supposed to bring misfortune to the one being glared at. Here the implication is that the contents of the basket represent that evil appearance or misfortune that seeks to bring harm on others.

The description of the basket's contents becomes clearer in the verses that follow. The angel lifted a heavy lead cover off the basket. Zechariah peered inside and saw a woman seated there. The angelic messenger then explained what she represented: "This is Wickedness" (v. 8). The woman was evil personified. She represented an evil that seeks to create havoc throughout the world.

As bad as things were in Zechariah's day, they could have been worse. The angel "pushed [the woman] back into the basket and pushed its lead cover down on it" (v. 8). God was holding evil in check in Zechariah's day, and He is still doing the same today. As Paul told the believers in Thessalonica, "For the secret power of lawlessness is already at work; but the one who now holds it back will continue to do so till he is taken out of the way" (2 Thess. 2:7).

Zechariah watched as the basket holding this personification of evil was carried away. "Where are they taking the basket?" he wanted to know (Zech. 5:10). The answer given by the messenger to Zechariah is the key to this vision. "He replied, 'To the country of Babylonia to build a house for it. When the house is ready, the basket will be set there in its place'" (v. 11).

Evil was being taken back to "the country of Babylonia"—literally to "the land of Shinar." Shinar was the location of the city of Babylon (Gen. 10:10 NKJV). It's where the tower of Babel was built (Gen. 11:2–4). It's the place to which Nebuchadnezzar carried off the treasures of God's temple (Dan. 1:2 NKJV). Shinar is the region we know today as southern Iraq. And the word translated "house" is the Hebrew word *bayit*, the normal word for a dwelling or habitation.

Wickedness will return to call Babylon home!

BABYLON IN THE FUTURE

In the early 1980s, Saddam Hussein recognized the symbolic significance of ancient Babylon. One year after assuming control over Iraq, he began rebuilding the ancient city. His reconstruction project had nothing to do with a passion for history or archaeology. It had everything to do with uniting Iraqis and other Arabs against their two historical enemies—Iran and Israel—as his foreword to the booklet for the first and second "Babylon International Festivals" made clear:

> Old policies have always ignored the status of Babylon when they created psychological and scientific barriers between Iraqis and their leaders in ancient times. No one has ever mentioned the achievements of "Hammurabi," the founder of the first organized set of laws in human history. Or "Nebuchadnezzar," the national hero who was able to defeat

the enemies of the nation on the land of "Kennan" [i.e., Canaan] and to take them as prisoner of war to Babylon. What we need now is to increase awareness in this regard.[3]

Saddam Hussein is gone, and his project to rebuild Babylon ended with the Second Gulf War. But the site remains. So does its psychological importance. So do God's predictions that wickedness will one day return to Shinar.

How will God fulfill His prophecies about Babylon? He doesn't say, and that should give us pause. The Bible doesn't tell us who will rebuild Babylon, or how it will be rebuilt. But God is clear in announcing that the city where humanity first raised its fist in rebellion against Him will return for a final curtain call at the end of the age. Three details from the book of Revelation, however, do hint at how Babylon will rise to power one last time.

In Revelation 17–18 the apostle John announced the destruction of a city named "Babylon the Great." Though many have tried to find some symbolic or spiritual interpretation, it seems more reasonable to identify the city with the prophecies of Babylon's destruction found in Isaiah, Jeremiah, and Zechariah. John pictured Babylon as a woman who personifies evil, looking back to Zechariah's description of evil personified. John described her as seated on many waters and holding a cup, two descriptions that come right from the prophecy of Jeremiah. John also provided several new details.

Babylon Will Be Known for Its Wealth

In Revelation 17:4 and 18:16, John described Babylon as a city dressed in "purple and scarlet, and . . . glittering with gold, precious stones and pearls." In 18:12–13, he listed these items, along with others, as "cargoes." The Greek word used refers specifically to the lading or freight of a ship.[4] Babylon will be a destination for the "merchants of the earth" (18:11) looking to sell all their exotic wares.

At a time when the basic necessities of life will be so scarce it will take an entire day's wages for a normal worker to purchase a quart of wheat or three quarts of barley (Rev. 6:6 NKJV), Babylon will have money to spend on every sort of luxury. They will be importing

> cargoes of gold, silver, precious stones and pearls; fine linen, purple, silk and scarlet cloth; every kind of citron wood, and articles of every kind made of ivory, costly wood, bronze, iron and marble; cargoes of cinnamon and spice, of incense, myrrh and frankincense, of wine and olive oil, of fine flour and wheat; cattle and sheep; horses and carriages; and human beings sold as slaves. (Rev. 18:12–13)

Babylon Will Exert Economic Control over the Antichrist

The apostle John resolved a mystery from the Old Testament. The prophets Isaiah, Jeremiah, and Zechariah pictured Babylon as the end-time evil power God vows to judge. But in the book of Daniel, the final world power is Rome

(Dan. 2; 7; 9). In Revelation 17, John made clear that there are *two* major powers during the end times—one military and the other economic.

The revived Roman Empire is the dominant military power in the final days. When John first described this empire and its ruler, pictured in Revelation 13 as a beast, he said the world will cry out, "Who is like the beast? Who can wage war against it?" (v. 4). John was actually providing additional details about a beast described originally by Daniel more than six centuries earlier. Daniel said this final empire will "devour the whole earth, trampling it down and crushing it" (Dan. 7:23), again describing its military prowess.

But what about Babylon? John pictured Babylon as a woman who personifies evil, borrowing from the prophecy in Zechariah. But John then added one additional detail: Babylon is riding on the beast. Actually, John said this woman named Babylon sits "by [literally 'on'] many waters" (Rev. 17:1), "on a scarlet beast" (v. 3), and on the "seven heads" that are part of the beast (v. 9). The position of the woman doesn't refer to her *location*, but to her *control*. The angel said to John that the waters where the woman sits refer to "peoples, multitudes, nations and languages" (v. 15). She's not located *everywhere*; she exerts control over *everyone*! Later John said she "rules over the kings of the earth" (v. 18). But how could Babylon have power or dominion over the rulers of the world, including the Antichrist?

Her authority is economic, not military. Babylon exerts some sort of financial or commercial control over the rest of the world. We're not told the source of her wealth in the passage, but certainly the oil wealth of the Middle East is a reasonable possibility. And that would be even more likely should other competing energy supplies—such as those in Russia and Iran—become inaccessible.

Babylon Will Be Destroyed by the Antichrist

For a period of time, Babylon will exert economic control over the Antichrist. He needs what she controls, and he is forced to pay dearly for it. But in his ever-growing quest for world domination, this future leader will not allow such a situation to continue indefinitely. In his anger and resentment, he will plot Babylon's destruction. John described it this way:

> The beast and the ten horns you saw will hate the prostitute. They will bring her to ruin and leave her naked; they will eat her flesh and burn her with fire. (Rev. 17:16)

This future leader will turn his war machine against Babylon and annihilate her.

Why would the Antichrist destroy Babylon? Won't this create even greater economic problems for the world? Couldn't this further disrupt what will have already become a scene of utter chaos? Babylon's destruction will most certainly create greater hardship. Revelation 18 describes other world rulers, merchants, and sea captains weeping over the loss of the city that had been a source of revenue in otherwise hard times (18:9–19). So why would the Antichrist lead a coalition of nations against Babylon? John provided the answer in Revelation 17:17:

> For *God has put it into their hearts to accomplish his purpose*
> by agreeing to hand over to the beast their royal authority,
> *until God's words are fulfilled.* (italics added)

God is the one who announced Babylon would be destroyed, and He will make sure His words are fulfilled!

Babylon is destined to rise—and fall—again. By arranging the few pieces of the prophetic puzzle that are available, we can make a tentative suggestion as to how it will come about.

THE RISE OF BABYLON

Babylon will rise to power sometime after the destruction of the alliance of nations made up of Russia, Iran, Turkey, and other countries from North Africa. After their destruction Babylon will become an economic powerhouse that will exert strong financial control over the world. Perhaps this will involve an attempt to unite the remaining Arab countries of the Middle East and refashion an oil cartel that will hold the world hostage. That possible scenario certainly makes sense.

But one thing is certain. Babylon will rise again to play a role in end-time events until it is finally destroyed, as we learn will happen in Revelation 18:21:

> Then a mighty angel picked up a boulder the size of a large
> millstone and threw it into the sea, and said:

"With such violence
the great city of Babylon will be thrown down,
never to be found again."

As we watch the evening news, we sense the clashing kingdoms. In our conversations with friends and colleagues we detect the anxiety and uncertainty of our times. But we rest assured that God is in control and that His ultimate plans and purposes will not be thwarted. For there is still one more kingdom to be ultimately established—a kingdom that will have no end.

EIGHT

FAITH, NOT FEAR

*Of the greatness of his government and peace there will
be no end. He will reign on David's throne and over
his kingdom, establishing and upholding it with justice
and righteousness from that time on and forever. The
zeal of the LORD Almighty will accomplish this.*

—ISAIAH 9:7

We started our journey together through the Middle East
by observing Jesus and His disciples leaving the temple
court and ascending the Mount of Olives. Somewhere on that
hillside they paused as the disciples took in the magnificent
buildings—buildings that Jesus then announced would soon
lie in ruins. The Mount of Olives was a fitting and familiar
place for Jesus and His followers to meet and discuss the future.

Much happened here historically. But as Jesus reminded them, there is so much more to come.

Forty days after Jesus' resurrection, He again met His disciples atop this magnificent mountain just to the east of Jerusalem. Luke, the writer of the gospel bearing his name, as well as the book of Acts, chronicled for us that final, compelling scene, the last few moments of Jesus' time here on earth.

> He said to them: "It is not for you to know the times or dates the Father has set by his own authority. But you will receive power when the Holy Spirit comes on you; and you will be my witnesses in Jerusalem, and in all Judea and Samaria, and to the ends of the earth."
>
> After he said this, he was taken up before their very eyes, and a cloud hid him from their sight.
>
> They were looking intently up into the sky as he was going, when suddenly two men dressed in white stood beside them. "Men of Galilee," they said, "why do you stand here looking into the sky? This same Jesus, who has been taken from you into heaven, will come back in the same way you have seen him go into heaven." (Acts 1:7–11)

THE FINAL CLASH OF KINGDOMS

The current clash of kingdoms will only end when the words spoken by these two angels to Jesus' disciples are fulfilled . . . when Jesus returns to this earth, to the very location from which He left. That's when He will conquer the worldwide forces arrayed against Israel and establish His rightful rule over all the earth. At that time a new era will begin for this planet. Jesus will reign over the people of the earth!

But the Bible makes it clear that *confrontation* precedes the *coronation*. Before Jesus returns as king, the nations of the earth will clash violently, first against one another and then together against Israel. In this book we have traced some of the major conflicts that will define the period leading up to Jesus' return. Jesus predicted it would be a time of international upheaval, of "wars and rumors of wars"—a time when "nation will rise against nation, and kingdom against kingdom" (Matt. 24:6–7). As confusing as those days will appear to some, every action will be carefully choreographed and orchestrated to bring the world to the ultimate gathering place of the ages . . . Armageddon.

ARMAGEDDON UNLEASHED

The Bible refers to the final gathering place for the armies of the world as Armageddon—a transliteration of two Hebrew words referring to the hill of Megiddo in the Jezreel Valley. In terms of proportion and violence, nothing will compare in intensity to the campaign that will begin in this broad valley and end in the city of Jerusalem.

As the remaining armies of the earth gather to come against Jerusalem, they will be led by the Antichrist, who is himself empowered by Satan. It will be at Jerusalem where the decisive clash of kingdoms, ultimately between good and evil, will reach its climax, with the forces of evil seemingly assured of victory.

And that's when the supreme King makes His appearance:

> I saw heaven standing open and there before me was a white horse, whose rider is called Faithful and True. With justice he judges and makes war. His eyes are like blazing fire, and on his head are many crowns. He has a name written on him that no one knows but he himself. He is dressed in a robe dipped in blood, and his name is the Word of God. The armies of heaven were following him, riding on white horses and dressed in fine linen, white and clean. Coming out of his mouth is a sharp sword with which to strike down the nations. "He will rule them with an iron scepter." He treads the winepress of the fury of the wrath of God Almighty. On his robe and on his thigh he has this name written: KING OF KINGS AND LORD OF LORDS. (Rev. 19:11–16)

The final clash of kingdoms will unfold as the kings of the earth, led by the Antichrist, meet face-to-face with the King of kings, Jesus Christ, and His heavenly armies. But the battle is anything but an epic struggle. A command from Jesus, pictured as a "sharp sword" coming from His mouth, strikes down the invaders, completely annihilating their armies. Nothing will stand in Jesus' way when He returns to assume His rightful role as king.

HOPE AND PEACE

All these events could start to unfold at any time. The world stage is already being set. The level of instability, uncertainty, and tension across the globe is palpable. And it is matched by a shocking sense of helplessness, apathy, and indifference among Western world leaders. They appear unable or unwilling to stand against the very forces of evil that threaten the existence of civilization as we know it.

But Jesus has made a promise to those who have already pledged allegiance to Him as King—"I will come back and take you to be with me" (John 14:3). The any-moment return of Jesus Christ for His bride—the host of believers yet alive on planet Earth—is imminent. Once He comes for His followers— and He could come today—the program for the nations as described in this volume will click into motion with astounding certainty.

Quite naturally, we could live our lives in fear, wringing our hands in despair over the growing world crisis. But for those who have placed their trust in Jesus, that is no way to live, especially in light of all God has revealed to us in His Word. Instead, our confidence—just as it was for Abraham as he stared down at the destruction of Sodom—needs to be in God and in His sure Word of promise. Like Abraham, we need to remember God's description of what lies in the future so we can continue to trust in the One who holds all things together, even when it might appear to us that everything is falling apart. We must live by faith, not fear, as events unfold. Then we can stand and look up, knowing our salvation is near!

ONE FINAL DECISION

The events described in this book will come to pass because the predictions about the future originated with God. They aren't the hopes or fears of mere humans. Everything God has announced will happen because He is in control of history. But that reality also leaves you facing a difficult question. How do *you* fit into God's plan? When Jesus returns for His church, will He take you to be with Him in heaven? Do you know beyond any doubt that heaven is your final home?

After taking his readers on a prophetic journey "from here to eternity" in the book of Revelation, John turned to speak directly to those who might not be sure of their eternal destiny. "The Spirit [the Holy Spirit of God] and the bride [the new Jerusalem, called the bride in 21:9–10] say, 'Come!' And let the one who hears say, 'Come!' Let the one who is thirsty come; and let the one who wishes take the free gift of the water of life" (Rev. 22:17).

Have you ever responded to God's offer of eternal life?

All of us have broken God's commands. Paul said it this way in the book of Romans: "All have sinned and fall short of the glory of God" (Rom. 3:23). Because all of us have done things we know are wrong, we assume God will somehow "grade on the curve" and lower His standards for letting people into heaven.

But God never lowers His standards, which is why Paul said, "For the wages of sin is death" (Rom. 6:23). Only someone who is absolutely perfect (that is, Jesus Christ) would ever be good enough to get into heaven through his own ability.

God wants us to live with Him for eternity. But we have sinned, and a just and righteous God must judge sin. Amazingly, God provided a way to pay for our sin Himself so we could spend eternity with Him. "But God demonstrates his own love for us in this: While we were still sinners, Christ died for us" (Rom. 5:8). Jesus was the perfect God/man. He lived a perfect life, but then He died on the cross. And while Jesus hung on the cross, He took upon Himself the punishment for our wrongdoings.

The entrance requirement to heaven is absolute perfection—a price none of us is able to pay. But God Himself paid that price, and now He is offering eternity to you as a free gift. That's why the Spirit and the bride say, "Come!" God has already paid the price to purchase eternal life for you. All you need to do is "take the free gift of the water of life."

How can you receive eternal life right now? First, acknowledge to God that you have sinned and can't get into heaven through your own good efforts. Second, accept as true the fact that Jesus Christ, God's eternal Son, became a man and died on the cross to pay for *your* sins. The fact that He rose from the dead proves His payment was sufficient. Third, trust in Jesus Christ for your eternal destiny. Place your hope for eternal salvation in Him. You can do this right now by praying a simple prayer such as this:

Dear Lord,

I know I've done wrong and fallen short of Your perfect ways. I realize my sins have separated me from You. I believe You sent Your Son, Jesus Christ, to earth to die on the cross for my sins. I now turn to Jesus and put my trust in what He did on the cross as payment for my sins. Please forgive me, and give me eternal life. Amen.

If you just prayed that prayer in sincerity, you have entered God's eternal family! God promised that all who put their trust in Jesus Christ as their Savior will receive eternal life.

For God so loved the world that he gave his one and only Son, that whoever believes in him shall not perish but have eternal life. (John 3:16)

You can depend on God to keep His promise!

If you did just say that prayer, we want to end with two final suggestions. First, begin reading the Bible. Start in the New Testament in the Gospel of John and read more about the one who died to pay for your sins. Second, try to find a good church in your area that believes and teaches the Bible. A church is *not* a gathering place for perfect people. It's a spiritual hospital where hurting people go to be mended spiritually. Tell the pastor about the decision you made, and ask him for guidance in helping you grow as a Christian.

AND IN CONCLUSION

The road from Jericho to Jerusalem snakes through the Judean wilderness on a steep uphill trajectory toward the Mount of Olives. The drive today takes just over thirty minutes, though it was a long day's walk in Bible times. That journey over the Mount of Olives also serves as a metaphor of Jesus' two arrivals in Jerusalem—one past and one still future.

In the past, the Judean wilderness was the place where "John the Baptist came, preaching in the wilderness of Judea" (Matt. 3:1). His message fulfilled a prediction from the prophet Isaiah: "A voice of one calling in the wilderness, 'Prepare the way for the Lord, make straight paths for him'" (v. 3).

Jesus came to fulfill many of the predictions found in the Old Testament. Most dramatically, He rode down the Mount of Olives into Jerusalem "on a colt, the foal of a donkey" just as the prophet Zechariah had predicted (Zech. 9:9; cf. Matt. 21:5). But His ultimate destination during His first coming was not to a coronation but to a cross. The crown He received was a crown of thorns.

The prophet Zechariah also predicted a second arrival on the Mount of Olives for Israel's Messiah. This time the Messiah's journey doesn't take Him through the wilderness. Instead, He will descend in triumph from heaven itself as Israel's victorious king.

> Then the LORD will go out and fight against those nations,
> as he fights on a day of battle. On that day his feet will stand

on the Mount of Olives, east of Jerusalem, and the Mount of Olives will be split in two from east to west, forming a great valley, with half of the mountain moving north and half moving south. (Zech. 14:3–4)

Jesus came the first time as the Lamb of God to take away the sin of the world, but He is coming back again—this time as the lion of the tribe of Judah, who will rule the nations with a rod of iron.

In this book we have explored some of the major events God has said will occur just before Christ's return. It's this still-future return—His second coming—when the strains of Handel's "Hallelujah Chorus," taken directly from Revelation 11:15, will finally be fulfilled.

The kingdom of this world is become the kingdom of our Lord and of his Christ, and He shall reign for ever and ever.

ACKNOWLEDGMENTS

We wish to express our gratitude to the many people who have made this book possible. First, our thanks go to David Moberg, senior vice president and group publisher at HarperCollins Christian Publishing, for his initial interest and for pointing us in the right direction. Thank you, David. Thank you also to Brian Hampton, senior vice president and publisher at Nelson Books for his enthusiastic support and his prayerful understanding in providing an extension during a personally difficult time in Mark's family life. We are especially thankful for Webster Younce, our editor and the associate publisher at Nelson Books, for his enthusiasm for the project that never waned (in spite of his becoming a new dad!) and for his careful editorial eye in making certain the message hit the mark for our readers. We also wish to thank the many team members at Thomas Nelson, from editorial, to author relations, to sales and marketing, to cover design and beyond, who collectively made our ideas and thoughts come to life through their amazing creative energy and talent. Finally, we wish to thank our wives: Kathy Dyer, for her excellent proofreading work all along the way and always gracious willingness to loan Charlie out for yet another collaboration. And to Tracy Tobey, for her loving and supportive help and understanding. Both Kathy and Tracy gave up significant time and attention as we worked our way through the project. May God be glorified in this finished work.

NOTES

Introduction

1. Peter Goodman, "Turbulence and Uncertainty for the Market After 'Brexit,'" *New York Times*, June 23, 2016, http://www .nytimes.com/2016/06/25/business/international/brexit -financial-economic-impact-leave.html.
2. Michael Birnbaum, William Branigin, and Sarah Kaplan, "Truck Rams Bastille Day Crowd in Nice, France, Killing at Least 84," *Washington Post*, July 15, 2016, https://www .washingtonpost.com/world/europe/truck-rams-bastille-day -crowd-in-southern-france/2016/07/14/18772ce6-4a0d-11e6 -bdb9-701687974517_story.html.
3. "Turkey: Mass Arrests After Coup Bid Quashed, Says PM," BBC News, July 16, 2016, http://www.bbc.com/news/world- europe-36813924.
4. Felicia Schwartz, "U.S., Russia Agree on Steps Designed to End War in Syria, but Details Sketchy," *Wall Street Journal*, July 16, 2016, http://www.wsj.com/articles/u-s-russia-agree-on-steps -designed-to-end-war-in-syria-but-details-sketchy-1468656368.
5. Ryan Browne, "Kerry: US, Russia to Cooperate Against al

Qaeda in Syria," CNN, July 15, 2016, http://www.cnn.com /2016/07/15/politics/kerry-us-russia-syria-al-nusra/index.html.

6. Zeina Karam and Vivian Salama, "Amid Russian Airstrikes, a Putin Craze Takes Hold in Mideast," Associated Press, October 12, 2015, http://www.msn.com/en-us/news/world /amid-russian-airstrikes-a-putin-craze-takes-hold-in-mideast /ar-AAfn2tI.

7. Jennifer LeClaire, "Why So Many People Think Obama Is the Antichrist," *CharismaNews*, August 7, 2015, http://www .charismanews.com/opinion/watchman-on-the-wall/50914 -why-so-many-people-think-obama-is-the-antichrist. Jennifer cites a poll from Public Policy Polling in which one in five Republicans believe President Obama is the Antichrist. For more detailed information on that poll, see "Democrats and Republicans Differ on Conspiracy Theory Beliefs," Public Policy Polling, April 2, 2013, http://www.publicpolicypolling .com/main/2013/04/conspiracy-theory-poll-results-.html.

Chapter 1: The Problem of Nations

1. Benjamin Netanyahu, *A Durable Peace: Israel and Its Place Among the Nations* (New York: Warner Books, 2000), xix.

2. Szu Ping Chan, "Brexit the 'Tip of the Iceberg' as Vote Risks EU's Destruction," *Telegraph* (UK), June 26, 2016, http://www .telegraph.co.uk/business/2016/06/26/brexit-the-tip-of-the -iceberg-as-vote-risks-eus-destruction/.

3. J. Dwight Pentecost, *Will Man Survive?: The Bible Looks at Man's Future* (Grand Rapids: Zondervan, 1980), 116.

Chapter 3: After ISIS

1. Graeme Wood, "What ISIS Really Wants," *Atlantic*, March 2015, http://www.theatlantic.com/magazine/archive /2015/03/what-isis-really-wants/384980/.

2. President Obama's Statement to the Nation on ISIL,

September 10, 2014. He said, "Now let's make two things clear: ISIL is not 'Islamic.' No religion condones the killing of innocents. And the vast majority of ISIL's victims have been Muslim. And ISIL is certainly not a state." See Chelsea Schilling, "Obama: Islamic State Is 'Not Islamic,'" WND, September 10, 2014, http://www.wnd.com/2014/09/obama-isis -is-not-islamic/.

3. David Remnick, "Going the Distance: On and Off the Road with Barack Obama," *New Yorker*, January 27, 2014, http:// www.newyorker.com/magazine/2014/01/27/going-the-distance -david-remnick. President Obama's exact quotation was, "The analogy we use around here sometimes, and I think is accurate, is if a jayvee team puts on Lakers uniforms that doesn't make them Kobe Bryant."

4. "CHP Deputies Walk Out of Parliament over Speaker's Secularism Remarks," *Hürriyet Daily News*, May 20, 2016, http://www.hurriyetdailynews.com/chp-deputies-walk-out-of -parliament-over-speakers-secularism-remarks.aspx?pageID =238&nID=99426&NewsCatID=338.

5. "Putin Calls Collapse of Soviet Union 'Catastrophe,'" *Washington Times*, April 26, 2005.

Chapter 4: Duplicitous Iran

1. Frank-Walter Steinmeier, quoted in Joseph Nasr and Paul Carrel, "Germany Sees Iran as Key to Stabilizing the Middle East," Reuters, January 19, 2016, http://www.reuters.com /article/us-mideast-crisis-germany-idUSKCN0UX1NG.

2. Hossein Salami, quoted in "IRGC General: Western Civilization on the Wane," *Iran Front Page*, May 31, 2016, http://ifpnews.com/news/politics/security/2016/05/irgc-general -western-civilization-on-the-wane/.

3. Hossein Askari, *Conflicts and Wars: Their Fallout and Prevention* (New York: Palgrave MacMillan, 2012), 120–23.

Askari put the estimated budgetary cost at $329 billion but admitted this didn't include postwar military expenditures or war financing costs. When those costs were added in, the total ballooned to $637 billion.

4. Vali Nasr, *The Shia Revival: How Conflicts Within Islam Will Shape the Future* (New York: W. W. Norton, 2006), 24.

5. Sadek Zibakalam, quoted in Saud al-Zahed, "Hatred of Arabs Deeply Rooted in Persians, Says Iranian Intellectual," *Al Arabiya News*, June 11, 2016, http://www.alarabiya.net/articles/2011/10/09/170927.html.

6. John Limbert, "Why Can't Arabs and Iranians Just Get Along?" *Foreign Policy*, December 1, 2010, http://foreignpolicy.com/2010/12/01/why-cant-arabs-and-iranians-just-get-along-2/.

7. Justin Siberell, special briefing, "Country Reports on Terrorism 2015," US Department of State, Washington, DC, June 2, 2016, http://www.state.gov/r/pa/prs/ps/2016/06/258013.htm.

8. Elise Labott, "John Kerry: Some Sanctions Relief Money for Iran Will Go to Terrorism," CNN Politics, January 21, 2016, http://www.cnn.com/2016/01/21/politics/john-kerry-money-iran-sanctions-terrorism/index.html.

9. Quoted in Ehud Yaari, "How Iran Plans to Destroy Israel," *American Interest* 11 (August 1, 2015): 1–2, http://www.the-american-interest.com/2015/08/01/how-iran-plans-to-destroy-israel/.

10. J. Weston Phillen, "Iran's Message on a Missile," *Atlantic*, March 2016, http://www.theatlantic.com/international/archive/2016/03/iran-missile-test/473013/.

11. "Iran Propaganda Clip Shows What a Muslim Invasion of Israel Would Look Like," *Jerusalem Post*, August 19, 2015, http://www.jpost.com/Arab-Israeli-Conflict/Iranian-propaganda-clip-shows-what-a-Muslim-invasion-of-Israel-would-look-like-412589.

12. Daniel J. Roth, "In Pictures: Thousands of Iranian Soldiers Stage Mock Siege of Temple Mount," *Jerusalem Post*,

November 21, 2015, http://www.jpost.com/Middle-East/Iran
/Report-Thousands-of-Iranian-soldiers-stage-mock-siege-of
-Temple-Mount-434845.

Chapter 5: Picking Up the Pieces

1. "Considering a Northern European Alliance," Stratfor,
   November 18, 2015, https://www.stratfor.com/sample
   /geopolitical-diary/considering-northern-european-alliance.
2. "The EU's Deal with Turkey Exposes the Moral Vacuum at Its
   Heart," *Spectator*, March 12, 2016, http://www.spectator
   .co.uk/2016/03/turkey-is-blackmailing-the-eu/.
3. Emre Peker, "With Brexit Turkey Loses Its Biggest Champion
   in Europe," *Wall Street Journal*, June 24, 2016, http://www.wsj
   .com/articles/with-brexit-turkey-loses-its-biggest-champion
   -in-europe-1466772772.
4. Garret Martin, "Europe's North-South Divide—a Stubborn
   Chasm," European Institute, August 2012, http://www
   .europeaninstitute.org/index.php/155-european-affairs/ea
   -august-2012/1614-europes-north-south-dividea-stubborn
   -chasm.
5. "Survey: Certified Divorce Financial Analyst (CDFA)
   Professionals Reveal the Leading Causes of Divorce," Institute
   for Divorce Financial Analysts, https://www.institutedfa.com
   /Leading-Causes-Divorce/.
6. Pieter C. Emmer and Leo Lucassen, "Migration from the
   Colonies to Western Europe since 1800," European History
   Online, November 13, 2012, http://ieg-ego.eu/en/threads
   /europe-on-the-road/economic-migration/pieter-c-emmer
   -leo-lucassen-migration-from-the-colonies-to-western-europe
   -since-1800.
7. Aaron Brown, "'Just Wait . . .' Islamic State Reveals It Has
   Smuggled Thousands of Extremists into Europe," *Express*
   (UK), November 19, 2015, http://www.express.co.uk/news

/world/555434/Islamic-State-ISIS-Smuggler-THOUSANDS
-Extremists-into-Europe-Refugees.

8. Raf Casert, "EU President: 'The Risk of Break-Up Is Real,'"
Business Insider, February 15, 2016, http://www.businessinsider
.com/ap-eu-future-not-what-it-once-was-with-2-big-crises-at
-summit-2016-2.

9. In both Daniel 7 and Revelation 13, the prophets describe a
beast having ten horns arising from the sea that brutalizes
the world and persecutes God's people for "a time, times, and
half a time" (Dan. 7:25), or "forty-two months" (Rev. 13:5)
until finally being destroyed by the Lord (Dan. 7:26; Rev.
19:20). While some believe these predictions pointed to Rome's
destruction of Jerusalem in AD 70, John didn't write the book
of Revelation until twenty-five years after that event, during
the reign of Domitian (Eusebius, *Church History* 3.18.1–3). He
wasn't writing history but presenting additional details about
Daniel's still-future prophecy.

10. Leon Wood, *A Commentary on Daniel* (Grand Rapids:
Zondervan, 1973), 71.

Chapter 6: Israel

1. Arnold Fruchtenbaum, *Israelology: The Missing Link in
Systematic Theology* (Tustin, CA: Ariel Ministries Press, 1993).

2. "UN Adopts 20 Resolutions Against Israel, 3 on Rest of the
World," UN Watch, November 25, 2015, http://www.unwatch.org
/un-to-adopt-20-resolutions-against-israel-3-on-rest-of-the-world/.

3. Eric R. Mandel, "Is the United Nations Anti-Semitic?" *Jerusalem
Post,* July 7, 2014, http://www.jpost.com/Opinion/Op-Ed
-Contributors/Is-the-United-Nations-anti-Semitic-361842.

4. Sarah Moughty, "Michael Oren: Inside Obama-Netanyahu's
Relationship," *Frontline,* January 6, 2016, http://www.pbs.org
/wgbh/frontline/article/michael-oren-inside-obama-netanyahus
-relationship/.

5. Matthew Duss, "How Is the Paris Peace Conference Different from All Other Peace Conferences?" *Tablet*, June 6, 2016. No longer accessible online.

6. Harold Hoehner, *Chronological Aspects of the Life of Christ* (Grand Rapids: Zondervan, 1977), 139.

7. Moti Bassok, "Poll: Fewer Than Half of Israelis See Themselves as Secular," *Haaretz*, September 13, 2010, http://matzav.com /poll-fewer-than-half-of-israelis-see-themselves-as-secular/.

Chapter 7: A Woman in a Basket

1. Robert Orttung, "Russia as an Energy Power Between Europe, the Middle East, and Asia," PONAIRS Eurasia Policy Memo No. 83, September 1, 2009, http://www.ponarseurasia.org/sites /default/files/policy-memos-pdf/pepm_083.pdf.

2. Simone Tagliapietra and Georg Zachmann, "Iran: A New Natural Gas Supplier for Europe?" *Bruegel*, October 5, 2015, http://bruegel.org/2015/10/iran-a-new-natural-gas-supplier-for -europe/.

3. Quote attributed to Saddam Hussein in the Babylon International Festival brochure for September 22, 1987, Baghdad: Iraqi Ministry of Culture and Information, 1987.

4. Walter Bauer, William F. Arndt, and F. Wilbur Gingrich, *A Greek-English Lexicon of the New Testament*, s.v., *gomos*.

ABOUT THE AUTHORS

CHARLES DYER (B.A., Washington Bible College; Th.M. and Ph.D., Dallas Theological Seminary) served as provost and dean of education at Moody Bible Institute before becoming Professor-at-Large of Bible at Moody and host of *The Land and the Book* radio program. Before coming to Moody, Dyer served for twenty years in multiple administrative and faculty roles at Dallas Theological Seminary, ultimately serving as executive vice president under Chuck Swindoll. Dyer is an Old Testament scholar and an authority on Middle Eastern history and geography. He also serves as associate pastor of Grace Bible Church in Sun City, Arizona. Charlie has traveled extensively throughout the Middle East for more than thirty years, leading more than eighty trips. He is the author of numerous books, including *The Rise of Babylon, A Voice in the Wilderness, What's Next?, The Christian Traveler's Guide, Character Counts: The Power of Personal Integrity,* and *Thirty*

Days in the Land with Jesus. He is also the coauthor of *Strike the Dragon* and *The ISIS Crisis* with Mark Tobey. Charlie and his wife, Kathy, have been married for more than forty years and have two grown children.

MARK TOBEY (B.A., Moody Bible Institute; Th.M., Dallas Theological Seminary) is a writer, editor, and former pastor. He formerly served as associate publisher and editor in chief at Moody Publishers in Chicago, where he also taught as an adjunct instructor of pastoral ministries in the undergraduate school. He presently serves as director of Charles R. Swindoll Product Development at Insight for Living Ministries in Frisco, Texas. He and his wife, Tracy, have four children and reside in north Texas.